# Building Assets Together

# 135 Group Activities for Helping Youth Succeed

## by Jolene L. Roehlkepartain
### Foreword by Dr. Peter L. Benson

## Dedication

To Eleanore Miller, who has always been interested in bringing out the best in me.

The development of this resource has been supported by grants from Lutheran Brotherhood, the Lilly Endowment, the W.K. Kellogg Foundation, the Blandin Foundation, and the Cargill Foundation. The research on developmental assets has been supported since 1989 by Lutheran Brotherhood, a Minneapolis-based fraternal benefits society that specializes in insurance, annuities, and investment products.

**Building Assets Together:**
**135 Group Activities for Helping Youth Succeed**
**by Jolene L. Roehlkepartain**
**Copyright © 1997 by Search Institute. Revised Edition**

*Practical research benefiting children and youth*

615 First Ave. N.E., Suite 125
Minneapolis, MN 55413
http://www.search-institute.org
Telephone: 612-376-8955
Toll Free: 800-888-7828
Fax: 612-376-8956
E-mail: search@search-institute.org

Printed on recycled paper in the United States of America.

10   9   8   7   6   5

Credits
**Editor:** Jennifer Griffin-Wiesner
**Book Design & Production:** Nancy Johansen-Wester
**Cover Photography:** Sal Skog

ISBN: 1-57482-336-1

# Table of Contents

Foreword by Dr. Peter L. Benson.................7

Introduction: Nurturing Developmental
Assets in Youth.............................8

How to Use this Book .......................11

## PART 1: UNDERSTANDING THE ASSET FRAMEWORK

### Chapter 1: Activities for the Eight Types of Assets .................................15

1. Worksheet: What Are Your Assets? ..........16
2. External Asset Category of Support: Support Web ..............................19
3. External Asset Category of Empowerment: Golden Nuggets .......................19
4. External Asset Category of Boundaries and Expectations: Boundary Signs...........20
5. External Asset Category of Constructive Use of Time: Time for What?.................20
6. Internal Asset Category of Commitment to Learning: Committed to Learning ...........21
7. Internal Asset Category of Positive Values: Values for All ...........................21
8. Internal Asset Category of Social Competencies: Worthwhile Role Models..22
9. Internal Asset Category of Positive Identity: Inflated or Deflated? .................22

### Chapter 2: Outside-the-Classroom Activities .................................23

10. Welcoming Places....................24
11. When Stress Hits.....................24
12. Community Assets....................25
13. Building Assets in Other Youth.................25
14. Success at Work ....................26
15. Give and Take ......................26

## PART 2: EXTERNAL ASSETS

### Chapter 3: Support............................29

**Family Support (Asset #1)**

16. Wall of Support.....................30
17. Classroom Census ..................30

18. Worksheet: The Ups and Downs of Support.............................31

**Positive Family Communication (Asset #2)**

19. A Letter to Mom and Dad ........................32
20. The Family History of Talk .....................32
21. Worksheet: Conversation Topics. .............33

**Other Adult Relationships (Asset #3)**

22. Whom Do You Go To?...............34
23. Who Supports You?.................34
24. Worksheet: The Adults Around You .........35

**Caring Neighborhood (Asset #4)**

25. Important Contact ...................36
26. Communication Roll.................36
27. Worksheet: Draw Your Neighborhood......37

**Caring School Climate (Asset #5)**

28. School Pride ........................38
29. School Census......................38
30. Worksheet: School Wish List ..................39

**Parent Involvement in Schooling (Asset #6)**

31. Talk Show Debate...................40
32. Pass and Talk ......................40
33. Worksheet: Getting Your Parents Involved................................41

### Chapter 4: Empowerment....................43

**Community Values Youth (Asset #7)**

34. Perceptions of Community Perceptions ...44
35. Community Cafeteria................44
36. Worksheet: The Valuable You.................45

**Youth as Resources (Asset #8)**

37. Big Brothers, Big Sisters..........................46
38. Activity Proposal....................46
39. Worksheet: Important Roles ..................47

**Service to Others (Asset #9)**

40. Penny Power .......................48
41. Random Acts of Service ..........................48
42. Worksheet: A Contract to Serve..............49

**Safety (Asset #10)**

43. Safe—or Not?........................50

44. Safety in Numbers ....................................50

45. Worksheet: Top Five .................................51

## Chapter 5: Boundaries and Expectations............................................53

### Family Boundaries (Asset #11)

46. Can of Worms .........................................54

47. Evolving Role Play ...................................54

48. Worksheet: At Which Age?........................55

### School Boundaries (Asset #12)

49. "If I Set the School Rules!" ........................56

50. Unclear Boundaries .................................56

51. Worksheet: Ideal School Boundaries........57

### Neighborhood Boundaries (Asset #13)

52. How Would You Respond? .........................58

53. The Ideal Neighborhood...........................58

54. Worksheet: Neighbors Who Keep a Close Eye ..............................................59

### Adult Role Models (Asset #14)

55. Following the Leader.................................60

56. Celebrities and Newsmakers ....................60

57. Worksheet: Role Models in Your Life. ......61

### Positive Peer Influence (Asset #15)

58. Media Review ..........................................62

59. Friendship Verse........................................62

60. Worksheet: Model Photo Album ..............63

### High Expectations (Asset #16)

61. Living with Expectations...........................64

62. Inspirational Sayings ................................64

63. Worksheet: Say What? ..............................65

## Chapter 6: Constructive Use of Time..67

### Creative Activities (Asset #17)

64. The Arts Around You................................68

65. Artistic Try-On. ........................................68

66. Worksheet: Opening Yourself Up to Creativity...........................................69

### Youth Programs (Asset #18)

67. School Activity Hunt................................70

68. Involvement in Activities .........................70

69. Worksheet: Essential Extracurricular Activities.................................................71

### Religious Community (Asset #19)

70. Role Models ............................................72

71. Yellow Pages Search ................................72

72. Worksheet: What About Your Involvement? ..........................................73

### Time at Home (Asset #20)

73. Pros and Cons..........................................74

74. Balancing Act...........................................74

75. Worksheet: Time Spent ............................75

## PART 3: INTERNAL ASSETS

## Chapter 7: Commitment to Learning..79

### Achievement Motivation (Asset #21)

76. Motivating Walk.......................................80

77. Thinking About Teachers .........................80

78. Worksheet: Bumper Sticker Messages .....81

### School Engagement (Asset #22)

79. What's Great?...........................................82

80. The Best of the Best .................................82

81. Worksheet: Learning Acrostic...................83

### Homework (Asset #23)

82. Homework Centers....................................84

83. Brainstorm Clouds ...................................84

84. Worksheet: Homework Pie........................85

### Bonding to School (Asset #24)

85. The Benefits of Caring...............................86

86. School Ratings ..........................................86

87. Worksheet: Your School ............................87

### Reading for Pleasure (Asset #25)

88. Oodles of Reading. ...................................88

89. Different Books for Different Folks...........88

90. Worksheet: Your Favorite Books ..............89

## Chapter 8: Positive Values ..................91

### Caring (Asset #26)

91. Helping Hands ........................................92

92. Caring for Others ...................................92

93. Worksheet: Helping Coupons..................93

**Equality and Social Justice (Asset #27)**

94. Pictures of Injustice ...................................94

95. Pizza Party ...............................................94

96. Worksheet: That's Not Fair! ....................95

**Integrity (Asset #28)**

97. Opinions Count........................................96

98. Classroom Continuum............................96

99. Worksheet: A Model of Integrity. .............97

**Honesty (Asset #29)**

100. 20 Questions.. ..........................................98

101. Fudging the Truth ...................................98

102. Worksheet: Your Honesty Policy..............99

**Responsibility (Asset #30)**

103. Taking Charge ........................................100

104. Character Comparison............................100

105. Worksheet: Places of Responsibility .......101

**Restraint (Asset #31)**

106. Listening to the Lyrics ............................102

107. Well, I'd Never! ......................................102

108. Worksheet: Why Wait? ..........................103

**Chapter 9: Social Competencies ........105**

**Planning and Decision Making (Asset #32)**

109. Decision Road Map.................................106

110. Toothpick Challenge ...............................106

111. Worksheet: Daily Planner........................107

**Interpersonal Competence (Asset #33)**

112. Paper Bag Skits........................................108

113. Active Listening ......................................108

114. Worksheet: Your Relationship Skills ......109

**Cultural Competence (Asset #34)**

115. A New Taste............................................110

116. Out vs. In..............................................110

117. Worksheet: Contact with Other Cultures..111

**Resistance Skills (Asset #35)**

118. Resisting Danger.....................................112

119. The Power of Resistance........................112

120. Worksheet: Say Yes to Saying No..........113

**Peaceful Conflict Resolution (Asset #36)**

121. Peacemakers Around Us .........................114

122. Dealing with World Conflict...................114

123. Worksheet: Rewriting Your History .......115

**Chapter 10: Positive Identity ............117**

**Personal Power (Asset #37)**

124. Disaster Control ......................................118

125. Pointing Fingers .....................................118

126. Worksheet: A Powerful Memo ...............119

**Self-Esteem (Asset #38)**

127. Messages.................................................120

128. Self-Esteem Notes ..................................120

129. Worksheet: What's Great About Me .......121

**Sense of Purpose (Asset #39)**

130. Passionate People....................................122

131. Redefining Success..................................122

132. Worksheet: A Meaningful Gift................123

**Positive View of Personal Future (Asset #40)**

133. A Look to the Future ...............................124

134. Nudge Your Neighbor .............................124

135. Worksheet: Your Dream of Your World ..125

**Additional Asset-Promoting Resources from Search Institute .............................126**

**About the Author ...................................127**

**About Search Institute ..........................127**

**40 Developmental Assets ......................128**

# Foreword

**by Dr. Peter L. Benson**
**President, Search Institute**

**W**hen I wrote *The Troubled Journey: A Portrait of 6th-12th Grade Youth*[1] in 1990, I don't think I realized its potential. In that report, we outlined 30 "developmental assets" that are important to helping young people grow up healthy, principled, and caring. Building on a foundation of research on adolescent development and needs, the report broke new ground in presenting a bold vision for youth in the United States—a vision that is met by only a small percentage of the hundreds of thousands of middle and high school youth we've surveyed.

These "developmental assets" are at the heart of the vision of helping young people grow up healthy, caring, and principled: positive relationships, opportunities, commitments, values, and competencies. We recently expanded the framework to 40 assets and are surveying 6th- to 12th-grade youth nationwide with this expanded framework. Ideally, each young person would experience most of these assets each and every day. Unfortunately, we find that the majority of 6th- to 12th-grade students we survey experience only about 18 of the 40.

As people have discovered this framework and the need, they are inspired, energized, and challenged. Parents see their parenting task in new ways. Educators think about school and their work differently. Religious leaders see new opportunities and challenges for their congregations. Youth-serving organizations are reshaping their programs. Government leaders are rethinking how they provide services. Community activists and influencers are reenergized.

In the midst of all the interest in asset building, people have started asking, "So, how do we build these assets? What can we do to make a difference for our own youth in our community?" The research reports are interesting to some, but people want more practical resources that guide them in making a concrete difference in the lives of youth.

We have published *Building Assets Together* as one response to that need. (Other resources are noted at the end of the book.) This book gives people who work with youth (teachers, youth workers, volunteers) hands-on activities and worksheets to use in introducing youth to the assets and in helping them discover their ability and responsibility to nurture their own assets—and the assets of those around them.

We are still learning more about assets and how to build them, and we continue to work on developing more resources and services to meet your needs. In the meantime, we hope the activities and worksheets will help you introduce and explore the assets with young people and help them in the process of nurturing their own assets.

---

[1] Peter L. Benson, *The Troubled Journey: A Portrait of 6th-12th Grade Youth* (Minneapolis, MN: Search Institute, 1993). First published in 1990 by Lutheran Brotherhood.

# Nurturing Developmental Assets in Youth

There seem to be at least three kinds of money managers in the world.

First are those you read about in personal finance books. They have a steady income and a well-thought-out budget. They balance their checkbook every month; they only charge what they can pay at the end of the month; they start saving for college when the baby arrives; and they think of every major purchase as an investment.

Other money managers, regardless of how much money they make, live paycheck to paycheck. Bills are paid when their bank balance isn't precariously low, and they put little thought into saving.

Then there is a third type. These money managers do their best to make ends meet but simply don't have the resources they need. They live paycheck to paycheck because they have to. Often they can't pay all their bills on time, and saving for the future just isn't feasible.

While most of us recognize the value of the first approach, the second and third pictures are disturbingly accurate analogies for the way our society has been taking care of our most valuable resource: our children and teenagers. Instead of doing everything we can to guarantee a good "return on our investment," we have spent tremendous amounts of energy just trying to recover from the damage that has already been done because we haven't chosen to—or couldn't—invest wisely in our youth. Oftentimes we don't have or know how to get the resources to help us understand what we can do to build a solid foundation for our youth.

It has become clear that a powerful approach for raising healthy young people is to invest energy and effort in "building assets" for and with them. This approach calls for shifting attention away from a crisis mentality that concentrates on stopping problems, to developing careful strategies that increase young people's exposure to positive and constructive relationships and activities that promote healthy, responsible, and compassionate choices.

## The Impact of Assets

Research underscores the importance of a focus on building assets. An ongoing research project of Search Institute has assessed the assets of 99,462 youth in 213 cities around the United States. This study has analyzed the presence and effect of 40 "developmental assets" in 6th- to 12th-grade youth.

In some ways, the assets represent commonsense priorities for helping youth grow up healthy. Twenty of the assets are external: interlocking systems of support, empowerment, boundaries and expectations, and constructive time use. The remaining 20 assets are internal: the commitments, values, skills, and identity that guide young people in their choices. (See Figure 1.) Many of them are things that people already talk about and do. What's unique about them, though, is that the framework of assets draws together many different pieces so that they are understandable and make sense together.

Furthermore, research underscores the incredible power of these assets in young people's lives. When young people have more of these developmental assets, they are much more likely to lead healthy, positive, productive lives. They simply do not make as many harmful decisions as youth who don't have these assets. They have fewer problems with alcohol and other drugs, violence, sexual involvement, and depression.

Figure 2 illustrates what happens when youth have more assets: Their unhealthy behaviors almost disappear and their positive behaviors increase. In short, increasing assets that young people experience decreases the crises they face, so the crises don't consume everyone's energy. Thus, by promoting assets, we spend less time fixing problems.

**Figure 1**

# 40 Developmental Assets

## EXTERNAL ASSETS

### Support
1. Family support
2. Positive family communication
3. Other adult relationships
4. Caring neighborhood
5. Caring school climate
6. Parental involvement in schooling

### Empowerment
7. Community values youth
8. Youth as resources
9. Service to others
10. Safety

### Boundaries and Expectations
11. Family boundaries
12. School boundaries
13. Neighborhood boundaries
14. Adult role models
15. Positive peer influence
16. High expectations

### Constructive Use of Time
17. Creative activities
18. Youth programs
19. Religious community
20. Time at home

## INTERNAL ASSETS

### Commitment to Learning
21. Achievement motivation
22. School engagement
23. Homework
24. Bonding to school
25. Reading for pleasure

### Positive Values
26. Caring
27. Equality and social justice
28. Integrity
29. Honesty
30. Responsibility
31. Restraint

### Social Competencies
32. Planning and decision making
33. Interpersonal competence
34. Cultural competence
35. Resistance skills
36. Peaceful conflict resolution

### Positive Identity
37. Personal power
38. Self-esteem
39. Sense of purpose
40. Positive view of personal future

## Rethinking Youth Work

On the one hand, these assets are easy to understand. Many teachers and youth workers have dedicated themselves to nurturing these experiences for and qualities within youth. But when we begin thinking about what it means to focus on building assets, it can completely change the way we think about working with youth. For example:

- Instead of focusing our time on lots of individual, negative problems that fragment our teaching plans or programming (such as violence, alcohol use, premature sexual activity), an asset-promoting approach focuses on nurturing positive relationships, opportunities, values, and skills that help youth make positive choices in all areas of life. We must still deal with some of the problem areas, but our efforts will be more focused and effective within the context of asset building.

- Instead of focusing on developing programs or teaching particular information, the asset-building approach focuses on nurturing relationships. Most assets are best developed in relationships—with parents, friends, neighbors, teachers, and other significant adults. Of course, many relationships are most effectively nurtured in the context of carefully structured programming or curriculum. But the structure is a means to an end, not the end in itself.

- Instead of focusing on immediate, short-term issues, an asset-promoting approach helps to focus thinking on long-term goals and opportunities.

- Instead of seeing youth as "the problem," young people become part of the solution. They have important roles to play in nurturing their own assets and the assets of their friends.

Figure 2

# The Power of Developmental Assets

| High-Risk Behavior Patterns | | Percent at Risk | | | | |
| --- | --- | --- | --- | --- | --- | --- |
| **Category** | **Definition** | **Total** | **If 0-10 Assets** | **If 11-20 Assets** | **If 21-30 Assets** | **If 31-40 Assets** |
| **Alcohol** | Three or more uses in past month and/or got drunk once or more in the past two weeks | **27%** | 53% | 30% | 11% | 3% |
| **Illicit Drugs** | Three or more uses in past year | **18%** | 42% | 19% | 6% | 1% |
| **Sexual Activity** | Sexual intercourse three or more times in a lifetime | **18%** | 33% | 21% | 10% | 3% |
| **Antisocial Behavior and Violence** | Three or more acts of violence in the past year | **33%** | 61% | 35% | 16% | 6% |
| **School Problems** | Skipped school two or more days in the past month and/or has below a C average | **19%** | 43% | 19% | 7% | 2% |

| Positive Behaviors | | Percent Involved | | | | |
| --- | --- | --- | --- | --- | --- | --- |
| **Category** | **Definition** | **Total** | **If 0-10 Assets** | **If 11-20 Assets** | **If 21-30 Assets** | **If 31-40 Assets** |
| **School Success** | Gets mostly A's in school | **23%** | 7% | 19% | 35% | 53% |
| **Values Diversity** | Places high importance on getting to know people of other racial/ethnic groups | **56%** | 34% | 53% | 69% | 87% |
| **Maintains Good Health** | Pays attention to healthy nutrition and exercise | **52%** | 25% | 46% | 69% | 88% |
| **Exhibits Leadership** | Has been a leader of a group or organization in the past year | **68%** | 48% | 67% | 78% | 87% |

Based on a sample of 99,462 6th- to 12th-grade public school youth in 213 towns and cities in the United States. Copyright © 1997 by Search Institute.

# How to Use This Book

**B**uilding *Assets Together* is a collection of group activities and worksheets that help young people explore their experiences with these 40 developmental assets. Through active and interactive learning, reflection, projects, and worksheets, young people learn about the importance of assets, strengths in their lives, sources of support, and areas for growth. Teaching young people about the assets helps them understand the important things they need to grow up healthy, empowering them to take charge and make positive choices for themselves and have a positive impact on the lives of others.

## Who This Book Is For

**P**eople in many settings have found the assets valuable in understanding and working with youth. Because of the broad audience, we have used language that we feel will be understood most widely. Furthermore, you may need or want to customize activities to fit your specific situation.

The activities have been developed to be useful to people who are involved with youth in schools, community organizations (recreation programs, clubs), and congregations (youth groups, religious education, retreats). Schools and communities that have surveyed their youth using *Search Institute's Profiles of Student Life: Attitudes & Behaviors* survey will find these activities particularly useful as they begin to explore and implement asset-promoting strategies.

The activities are designed to be used with 6th- to 12th-grade youth. Depending on the maturity and interests of the youth you work with, you may find some activities are more appropriate for youth younger than yours, while others may be more applicable to older youth. Adapt the activities to best meet the needs of your group of young people.

## Ways to Use This Book

**M**any of these activities can be completed in less than 30 minutes. They can be used in whatever format and combination best fit your needs. Here are some possibilities:

• They can stand alone in a series of activities, or they can be integrated into broader lessons or learning objectives.

• You can pick and choose individual activities. For example, you can use the first activity (where youth assess all the assets) as an introduction, then choose follow-up activities that best address the concerns and issues raised.

• You may choose to systematically use an activity on each asset throughout a school or program year. (Activities 1-9 can work together to provide a helpful overview of the asset framework and the eight asset categories.)

• Or, if your school or community has surveyed young people's assets using *Profiles of Student Life: Attitudes & Behaviors*, you may choose to select activities that address strengths or gaps in your youths' assets.

## How the Book Is Organized

**B**uilding *Assets Together* is organized around the framework of developmental assets. It begins with a self-analysis that introduces all 40 assets. Youth can see what 99,462 youth who have completed anonymous surveys that asked similar questions have said about their assets.

The next eight activities each deal with one of the eight general types of assets: support, empowerment, boundaries and expectations, constructive use of time, commitment to learning, positive values, social competencies, and positive identity. Activities 10 through 15 are outside-the-classroom activities focusing on all 40 assets. These activities are appropriate as field trips, homework assignments, and opportunities for community involvement.

The rest of the activities focus on each of the 40 assets with three activities for each asset. For each asset you'll find two experiential classroom activities and a worksheet that you can photocopy for your youth. If you wish, youth can collect these worksheets to create a notebook that includes their insights on all 40 assets.

These activities are designed to be positive experiences for youth. However, discussions of assets may evoke strong feelings and reactions, both positive and negative. Some activities could lead to difficult discussions, especially when using them with youth with few assets or with particularly vulnerable youth. Be sensitive to young people's concerns, and adapt the activities and reflection questions to fit your situation and your educational goals. Don't force youth to participate in any of these activities. Invite all youth to share their ideas and feedback about the assets and/or the activities.

Building developmental assets is an important strategy for schools, youth-serving organizations, congregations, families, and communities. There are no instant ways to build them; they must be nurtured in many ways in relationships with many people. However, by using these activities with youth, you can help young people focus their thinking and priorities. In doing so, you can contribute in a significant way to helping them succeed—both now and in the future.

# PART 1
# Understanding the Asset Framework

# Chapter 1

# Activities for the Eight Types of Assets

The activities in this chapter help youth become familiar with what the assets are and why they are important. The first activity identifies the 40 developmental assets and asks youth to compare their own responses with those of 99,462 youth across the country. The following activities introduce the eight major types of assets: support, empowerment, boundaries and expectations, constructive use of time, commitment to learning, positive values, social competencies, and positive identity.

## What Are Your Assets?

**Focus:** Youth analyze their own assets and compare their response to those of 99,462 surveyed by Search Institute.

**#1**

**You will need:**
• copies of "An Asset Checklist" —one for each youth

Photocopy the worksheet "An Asset Checklist" (p. 17) for each youth to fill out. Assure them that no one will look at their sheets, so they can be honest with themselves. They will be asked only to share what they want to share. After youth finish, have them compare themselves to 99,462 youth nationwide (Figure 4). Then ask questions such as these:

1. Most young people experience many of these assets. The top four assets that most youth have in their lives are:
• #40-feeling optimistic about their personal futures (70%)
• #1-having a family life that provides high levels of love and support (64%)
• #19-being involved in a community of faith (64%)
• #22-being actively engaged in school and learning (64%)

How do your assets compare with those of other young people? In what ways are your assets similar to and different from youth surveyed by Search Institute? Why do you think that is?

2. Most young people are also missing certain other assets. The four assets that most youth do not have in their lives are:

• #17-spending three or more hours per week in lessons or practice in music, theater, or other arts (19%)
• #25-reading for pleasure three or more hours per week (24%)
• #7-perceiving that adults in the community value youth (20%)
• #5-seeing their school as providing a caring, encouraging environment (24%)

How many of these assets do you have in your life? How important do you think these assets are? Why? Why do you think researchers have said they are important in growing up healthy?

3. The assets are separated into internal assets and external assets. Assets #1-#20 are considered external assets: the support, empowerment, boundaries and expectations, and constructive activities that surround you. Assets #21-#40 are considered internal assets: the commitments, values, social competencies, and positive youth identity that help you make wise choices.

Do you have more internal assets or external assets? Why do you think that is?

4. Research shows that the average teenager has only about 18 of these assets. Look at how many assets you checked "true" for. How similar or different are you to other youth nationally? Also compare yourself to others in your grade and others of your gender (see box). Why do you think older youth have fewer assets compared with younger youth? Why do you think females have more assets than males?

**Figure 3**

# Assets by
# Grade and Gender

**In the study of 99,462 youth nationwide, the number of assets youth experience by grade and gender are as follows:**

| | |
|---|---|
| **All** | 18.0 |
| **Grade 6** | 21.5 |
| **Grade 7** | 19.8 |
| **Grade 8** | 17.8 |
| **Grade 9** | 17.4 |
| **Grade 10** | 16.9 |
| **Grade 11** | 16.9 |
| **Grade 12** | 17.2 |
| **Females** | 19.5 |
| **Males** | 16.5 |

# An Asset Checklist

**Many young people experience too few of the developmental assets. Check whether each statement is true or false to get an idea of areas where you experience a lot of assets and areas where you could use more assets.**

## EXTERNAL ASSETS

**True   False**

### Support
1. I receive lots of love and support from my family . . . . . . . . . . . . . . . . . . . . . . . . . . . . . .
2. My parent(s) and I communicate positively, and I am willing to go to my parent(s) for advice and counsel
3. I receive support from three or more nonparent adults . . . . . . . . . . . . . . . . . . . . . . . . . . .
4. I experience caring neighbors
5. My school provides a caring, encouraging environment . . . . . . . . . . . . . . . . . . . . . . . . . .
6. My parent(s) are actively involved in helping me succeed in school . . . . . . . . . . . . . . . . . .

### Empowerment
7. I believe that adults in my community value youth . . . . . . . . . . . . . . . . . . . . . . . . . . . . .
8. I believe that young people are given useful roles in my community . . . . . . . . . . . . . . . . . .
9. I serve in my community for one hour or more per week . . . . . . . . . . . . . . . . . . . . . . . . .
10. I feel safe at home, at school, and in the neighborhood . . . . . . . . . . . . . . . . . . . . . . . . . .

### Boundaries and Expectations
11. My family has clear rules and consequences, and monitors my whereabouts . . . . . . . . . . . .
12. My school provides clear rules and consequences . . . . . . . . . . . . . . . . . . . . . . . . . . . . . .
13. My neighbors take responsibility for monitoring young people's behavior . . . . . . . . . . . . . .
14. Parent(s) and other adults model positive, responsible behavior . . . . . . . . . . . . . . . . . . . .
15. My best friends model responsible behavior . . . . . . . . . . . . . . . . . . . . . . . . . . . . . . . . . .
16. Both my parent(s) and my teachers encourage me to do well . . . . . . . . . . . . . . . . . . . . . .

### Constructive Use of Time
17. I spend three hours or more per week in lessons or practice in music, theater, or other arts . . .
18. I spend three hours or more per week in sports, clubs, organizations at school, and/or in community organizations . . . . . . . . . . . . . . . . . . . . . . . . . . . . . . . . . . . . . . . . . . . . . .
19. I spend one or more hours per week in activities in a religious institution . . . . . . . . . . . . . .
20. I go out with friends "with nothing special to do," two or fewer nights per week . . . . . . . . . .

## INTERNAL ASSETS

### Commitment to Learning
21. I am motivated to do well in school . . . . . . . . . . . . . . . . . . . . . . . . . . . . . . . . . . . . . . .
22. I am actively engaged in learning . . . . . . . . . . . . . . . . . . . . . . . . . . . . . . . . . . . . . . . . .
23. I do at least one hour of homework every school day . . . . . . . . . . . . . . . . . . . . . . . . . . . .
24. I care about my school . . . . . . . . . . . . . . . . . . . . . . . . . . . . . . . . . . . . . . . . . . . . . . . .
25. I read for pleasure three or more hours per week . . . . . . . . . . . . . . . . . . . . . . . . . . . . . .

### Positive Values
26. I place a high value on helping other people . . . . . . . . . . . . . . . . . . . . . . . . . . . . . . . . .
27. I place a high value on promoting equality and reducing hunger and poverty . . . . . . . . . . . .
28. I act on my convictions and stand up for my beliefs . . . . . . . . . . . . . . . . . . . . . . . . . . . . .
29. I tell the truth even when it is not easy . . . . . . . . . . . . . . . . . . . . . . . . . . . . . . . . . . . . .
30. I accept and take personal responsibility . . . . . . . . . . . . . . . . . . . . . . . . . . . . . . . . . . . .
31. I believe it is important not to be sexually active or to use alcohol or other drugs . . . . . . . . . . . .

### Social Competencies
32. I know how to plan ahead and make choices . . . . . . . . . . . . . . . . . . . . . . . . . . . . . . . . . .
33. I have empathy, sensitivity, and friendship skills . . . . . . . . . . . . . . . . . . . . . . . . . . . . . . . .
34. I have knowledge of and comfort with people of different cultural/racial/ethnic backgrounds . .
35. I can resist negative peer pressure and dangerous situations . . . . . . . . . . . . . . . . . . . . . . .
36. I seek to resolve conflict nonviolently . . . . . . . . . . . . . . . . . . . . . . . . . . . . . . . . . . . . . .

### Positive Identity
37. I feel I have control over things that happen to me . . . . . . . . . . . . . . . . . . . . . . . . . . . . .
38. I have a high self-esteem . . . . . . . . . . . . . . . . . . . . . . . . . . . . . . . . . . . . . . . . . . . . . . .
39. I believe my life has a purpose . . . . . . . . . . . . . . . . . . . . . . . . . . . . . . . . . . . . . . . . . . .
40. I am optimistic about my personal future . . . . . . . . . . . . . . . . . . . . . . . . . . . . . . . . . . . .

**Figure 4**

# Developmental Assets Among American Youth

**Here are the percentages of 99,462 6th- through 12th-grade youth surveyed by Search Institute who report having each asset.**

| | | |
|---|---|---|
| 1. | I receive lots of love and support from my family. | 64% |
| 2. | My parent(s) and I communicate positively, and I am willing to go to my parent(s) for advice and counsel. | 26% |
| 3. | I receive support from three or more nonparent adults. | 41% |
| 4. | I experience caring neighbors. | 40% |
| 5. | My school provides a caring, encouraging environment. | 24% |
| 6. | My parent(s) are actively involved in helping me succeed in school. | 29% |
| 7. | I believe that adults in my community value youth. | 20% |
| 8. | I believe that young people are given useful roles in my community. | 24% |
| 9. | I serve in my community for one hour or more per week. | 50% |
| 10. | I feel safe at home, at school, and in my neighborhood. | 55% |
| 11. | My family has clear rules and consequences, and monitors my whereabouts. | 43% |
| 12. | My school provides clear rules and consequences. | 46% |
| 13. | My neighbors take responsibility for monitoring young people's behavior. | 46% |
| 14. | Parent(s) and other adults model positive, responsible behavior. | 27% |
| 15. | My best friends model responsible behavior. | 60% |
| 16. | Both my parent(s) and my teachers encourage me to do well. | 41% |
| 17. | I spend three hours or more per week in lessons or practice in music, theater, or other arts. | 19% |
| 18. | I spend three hours or more per week in sports, clubs, organizations at school, and/or in community organizations. | 59% |
| 19. | I spend one or more hours per week in activities in a religious institution. | 64% |
| 20. | I go out with friends "with nothing special to do," two or fewer nights per week. | 50% |
| 21. | I am motivated to do well in school. | 63% |
| 22. | I am actively engaged in learning. | 64% |
| 23. | I do at least one hour of homework every school day. | 45% |
| 24. | I care about my school. | 51% |
| 25. | I read for pleasure three or more hours per week. | 24% |
| 26. | I place a high value on helping other people. | 43% |
| 27. | I place a high value on promoting equality and reducing hunger and poverty. | 45% |
| 28. | I act on my convictions and stand up for my beliefs. | 63% |
| 29. | I tell the truth even when it is not easy. | 63% |
| 30. | I accept and take personal responsibility. | 60% |
| 31. | I believe it is important not to be sexually active or to use alcohol or other drugs. | 42% |
| 32. | I know how to plan ahead and make choices. | 29% |
| 33. | I have empathy, sensitivity, and friendship skills. | 43% |
| 34. | I have knowledge of and comfort with people of different cultural/racial/ethnic backgrounds. | 35% |
| 35. | I can resist negative peer pressure and dangerous situations. | 37% |
| 36. | I seek to resolve conflict nonviolently. | 44% |
| 37. | I feel I have control over things that happen to me. | 45% |
| 38. | I have a high self-esteem. | 47% |
| 39. | I believe my life has a purpose. | 55% |
| 40. | I am optimistic about my personal future. | 70% |

## Support Web

<u>Focus:</u> **Youth identify various sources of support in their lives.**

**External Asset Category: SUPPORT**

*You will need:*
- **a beach ball or other type of "blow-up" ball**
- **enough yarn to make a web**

Have youth sit in a circle. Give one youth a ball of yarn. Have that youth name one person who supports her or him and how. Then ask the youth to hold on to the end of the yarn and throw the rest of the ball to another person in the circle. The youth who catches the ball of yarn then holds onto the yarn and names a person who supports her or him and how before holding on to an end and throwing the ball of yarn to someone else. As the activity continues, a web that connects all the youth will appear. Make sure that all the youth get to participate at least once.

After a web has been spun and youth begin to run out of ideas, explain to young people that the ball represents young people and the web is the web of support made up of all of the people mentioned. Throw the ball into the web and encourage the youth to move it around without letting it slip through the gaps in the web. If the web cannot support the ball, continue adding to it until the ball bounces easily without falling through. Then stop and ask questions such as these:

- **How many different types of people did we name (e.g., family, friends, neighbors)?**

- **Is it more important to you to have lots of different people who are supportive or just a few who are very supportive? Why?**

- **What happens when the gaps in our webs of support are too wide?**

- **Which attributes do supportive people have that are important to you?**

- **In what ways do you support your friends and family?**

- **If someone you know seemed to need more support, how would you suggest that he or she find it?**

## Golden Nuggets

<u>Focus:</u> **Youth discuss how valued youth are in society and in their community.**

**External Asset Category: EMPOWERMENT**

*You will need:*
- **rocks of different sizes and shapes— one for each youth**

Have youth sit in groups of four. Give each youth a rock. Have youth compare rocks and decide which rock is the most valuable and which is the least valuable. Then have youth lay the rocks in a line that shows the order of importance. Have groups share how they determined which rocks were most valuable and why.

Then have youth pick up their original rocks. Tell them that each rock has gold inside, and each nugget of gold inside is unique. Have them again lay the rocks in a line that shows the order of importance.

Afterward ask questions such as these:

- **Was it more difficult to determine the value of the rocks based on what you could see on the outside or based on what you couldn't see on the inside? Why?**

- **In terms of judging people, how do we usually decide who's valuable and who's not? Are those the best ways to determine these things? Why or why not?**

- **Think about all the age groups in our society. Which age groups are most valued? Least valued? Why?**

- **Overall, how does our community do at valuing youth?**

- **Are youth in our community more likely to be viewed as valuable for what they are now, or for what they might become?**

- **What would you suggest needs to happen to encourage our community to value youth more?**

- **What steps can you take to ensure that young people are valued?**

## Boundary Signs

<u>Focus:</u> **Youth think about appropriate boundaries for their age.**

**You will need:**
- **markers**
- **many different colored large sheets of construction paper**
- **scissors**

### External Asset Category: BOUNDARIES AND EXPECTATIONS

Have youth look at items #11–#13 on their asset checklists (p. 17). Ask each youth to make a sign that looks like a traffic sign that sums up an appropriate boundary message they receive from either their family (asset #11), school (asset #12), or neighborhood (asset #13). Encourage youth to think of a familiar traffic sign (such as GO, YIELD, DO NOT ENTER, ONE WAY, CAUTION, STOP) and write that word at the top of their construction paper and then write a short message underneath that reflects an appropriate boundary for youth their age. For example, youth might write: "YIELD to other family members so everyone gets a chance to be heard," "CAUTION: Classmates who pressure you to take risks," or "GO meet one friendly neighbor and get to know her or him." Then have youth show and explain their signs. Ask:

- **What are the most common boundaries you experience? Do you experience different boundaries in different settings?**
- **Sometimes we don't like boundaries because they interfere with things we want to do. When are some times you've been glad you had boundaries?**
- **What are some boundaries you've experienced or heard of that are inappropriate? What could you do to question or challenge those boundaries in a respectful way?**
- **What happens when you don't have any boundaries? Why are they important for making good choices in life?**
- **The best boundaries are ones that give consistent messages between home, school, and your community. Which messages do you get that are consistent? Which are inconsistent?**
- **How do you make good choices when you are given inconsistent messages about boundaries?**

## Time for What?

<u>Focus:</u> **Youth tell about how they spend their time each day.**

**You will need:**
- **newsprint (at least 11 sheets)**
- **markers**
- **masking tape**

### External Asset Category: CONSTRUCTIVE USE OF TIME

Have teams of youth make each of the following signs (or others that are appropriate for your group): Sleep, Eat, School, Work, Homework, Extracurricular Activities, Religious Activities, Spend Time With Friends, Spend Time With Family, Have Alone Time, and Watch Television. Have youth hang each of these signs on the walls of your room using masking tape. Make sure the signs are spread throughout the room.

Then say something like: "Now, everyone stand in the middle of the room. I'm going to start naming hours of the day. Think about what you're doing at that time, and run to the appropriate sign and stand there until I name the time of day when you switch to something else. Ready? Let's begin.

"Pretend it's one minute past midnight on a Wednesday school night. Where are you? (Pause.) How about 1 a.m.? (Pause.) 2 a.m.? (Pause.) 3 a.m.? (Pause.)"

Continue naming each hour until you get back to midnight. Watch where youth go and congregate and for how long. Then repeat the activity, using a weekend day.

Then ask questions such as these:

- **Where do you spend most of your time on school days? Why?**
- **Where do you spend most of your time on the weekends? Why?**
- **Are there other things you spend lots of time doing that aren't included in the signs in this room? What are they?**
- **What kinds of activities do you do that are challenging and stimulating?**
- **What do you consider to be a big waste of time? Why?**
- **Which activities build the most assets for you? The least?**
- **If you could choose how much time you would spend on each activity, which activities would you shorten? Why? Which ones would you lengthen? Why?**

## Committed to Learning

**Focus:** Youth create slogans to encourage educational commitment.

### Internal Asset Category: COMMITMENT TO LEARNING

Form four teams. Give each team a piece of poster board, markers, pencils, and masking tape. Assign each team one of these assets:

- #21-I am motivated to do well in school.
- #22-I am actively engaged in learning.
- #23-I do at least one hour of homework every school day.
- #24-I care about my school.
- #25-I read for pleasure three or more hours per week.

Have each team create a catchy slogan to put on its poster board (think of it as a billboard) that reflects the asset the team has been given. For example, the team with #22 might write: "Be All You Can Be: Keep Learning Every Day." Encourage teams to be creative and spend time designing their posters. Have teams show their "billboards" to the whole group. Ask:

- **Which of these slogans is easiest for you to follow? Which is hardest? Why?**
- **Who are the people in your life who encourage you to keep learning?**
- **When you feel like giving up, what can you do to build up your commitment to learning?**

After the discussion, hang the billboards in your classroom, meeting room, or in the hallway.

**You will need:**
- **four sheets of poster board**
- **markers**
- **pencils**
- **masking tape**

## Values for All

**Focus:** Youth identify positive, negative, and controversial values.

### Internal Asset Category: POSITIVE VALUES

Ask for three volunteers. Give each volunteer a piece of chalk and a section of the chalkboard. Have one volunteer write "Positive Values" at the top of her or his section. Have the second volunteer write "Negative Values" at the top of her or his section. And have the third volunteer write "Controversial Values" at the top of her or his section. Ask the group to spend a few minutes discussing what the word "values" means. While there are several different definitions of the word, this activity focuses on beliefs or principles that guide people's actions and decisions

Then ask youth to name values and discuss which heading best fits each value. Ask the volunteers to write each value under the appropriate heading. If youth have trouble choosing a category for a particular value, suggest that they put it under "Controversial Values." For example, youth might say that "honesty," "respect," "equality," and "social justice" are all positive values. Youth may then say that "prejudice" and "greed" are negative values, and that "believing in abstinence for teenagers" and "having faith in a higher power" can be controversial, since some people value these things and others don't. Talk about the similarities and differences between these values. Ask:

- **Which types of values are hardest to think of? Which are easiest? What's different about them?**
- **Why are some values more controversial than others?**
- **Is it OK to disagree about which values are important?**
- **What do you think life would be like if we didn't have positive values?**
- **What does this tell us about the benefits of positive values?**

**You will need:**
- **chalkboard and chalk**
- **newsprint and markers**

## Worthwhile Role Models

**Focus:** Youth analyze the social competencies of positive role models.

**#8**

*You will need:*
- **four sheets of poster board**
- **markers**
- **pencils**
- **masking tape**

**Internal Asset Category:**
**SOCIAL COMPETENCIES**

Ask your group to name six real-life positive role models they look up to (make sure you have both females and males). Then have youth form small teams. Ask each team to pick one of the six role models and discuss that person. Have youth analyze that role model's social competencies by looking at assets #32 through #36. If youth wish to do more study, they could research magazine and newspaper articles about their role models and find out more about their personal habits, values, and skills. Then have a follow-up session where youth role-play the role models (emphasizing their social competencies) on a mock talk show.

After youth have identified the important competencies, ask:

- **Which competencies seem to be most common among these role models? Are there any competencies they need to develop more?**
- **In what ways do these competencies help our role models succeed?**
- **Which competencies do you think you already have? Which would you like to develop?**
- **If these role models were in the room with us, what do you think they would tell us about ways to build these competencies in ourselves?**

## Inflated or Deflated?

**Focus:** Youth symbolize how others affect their identity.

**#9**

*You will need:*
- **chalkboard and chalk or**
- **newsprint and markers**

**Internal Asset Category:**
**POSITIVE IDENTITY**

Give each youth a balloon. Tell them to blow once in the balloon each time you mention something that someone does that helps them feel good about themselves. Have youth let out a little air each time you mention something that makes them doubt or not feel good about themselves.

Use examples such as these:

- Someone takes your needs seriously.
- Someone gives you a hug.
- Someone laughs at your jokes.
- Someone takes advantage of you.
- Someone discriminates against you.
- Someone trusts you with a secret.
- Someone believes you can do something and tells you so.
- Someone rejects you.
- Someone thanks you for doing something for her or him.
- Someone expects too much of you and you can't meet those expectations.
- Someone calls you names.
- Someone you care about ignores you.
- Someone forgives you.
- Someone invites you to do something exciting.

After the activity, ask:

- **How did you feel when you saw your balloons become bigger? Smaller?**
- **Did some people deflate their balloons quietly while others did so loudly? Why? How is that like what you see people do in real life?**
- **Think about what your balloon would look like right now if I were to ask you inflate it to match the level of how you feel about yourself. Would it be large or small? Why?**
- **How can we encourage each other to keep our balloons large and full without popping?**

# Chapter 2

# Outside-the-Classroom Activities

The six activities in this chapter are designed to help youth explore assets outside the classroom. While they involve more extensive preparation and time, they can also be particularly valuable in bringing to life the idea of developmental assets.

## Welcoming Places

**Focus:** Youth survey the community for youth hangouts.

**You will need:**
• transportation for your group

**H**ave youth form four groups. Ask each group to tour your community to locate places where young people hang out. (Look for recreational areas, restaurants, parks, streets, organizations, and other places youth might go.) Have each group list what they learn about these places and rate whether each place is a good or bad place for young people to hang out.

After groups do this, have them compare their findings. Then ask questions such as:
• **Overall, do you think our community has enough positive places for young people to hang out? Why or why not?**
• **What concerns do you have about some of the places youth hang out? Why?**
• **What keeps our community from having positive places for youth to hang out? Why?**
• **What encourages our community to create more positive places for youth to hang out?**
• **What suggestions do you have to improve some of these youth hangouts?**
• **Does our community need more or fewer youth hangouts? Why?**

### Variation

Have youth compare hangouts for youth versus hangouts for younger children (from birth to age 11) versus hangouts for adults. To whom does your community seem to cater? Why do you think that is so?

## When Stress Hits

**Focus:** Youth examine the role of assets in difficult life situations.

**You will need:**
• transportation for your group

**A**s a group, visit a place where people are struggling with difficult life situations. Consider visiting a hospital, a battered women's shelter, an unemployment office, a homeless shelter, or a home for runaway youth. Talk about how every person encounters periods of stress and that the more assets you have, the better you can cope with these trying times. Before you visit, ask the youth to talk about how they can show respect for the people who are dealing with these difficult situations. Be clear about what kinds of actions or statements would be inappropriate.

At the place you visit, ask someone who works there questions such as:
• **Why do you think people come to your organization?**
• **Why do some people cope better with difficulty than others?**
• **What determines whether a person is able to get out of a difficult situation?**
• **What do you do to help people make positive changes in their lives? Why?**
• **What advice would you give so that people are less likely to find themselves in such trying circumstances?**

Afterwards talk about the following kinds of questions:
• **What were the most important things you heard or saw while we were visiting?**
• **What role do assets play in helping people deal with difficult situations?**
• **How can the information we heard help us better cope with difficulties when they arise in our lives?**

## Community Assets

<u>Focus:</u> **Youth identify high asset-building and low asset-building places in their community.**

**You will need:**

- copies of a map of your community —one for each youth
- two different colors of pens—one of each color for each youth
- transportation for your group

Copy a map of your community. Then tour your community by bus, van, or on foot. Stop at various points and, as a group, discuss whether each of these points are high asset-building areas or low asset-building areas and why. (For example, you could stop at a police station, a park, a religious congregation, a strip mall, city hall, a high-income residential area, a low-income residential area, a commercial area, etc.)

Have youth highlight the corresponding points on their map, using one color for high asset-building areas, and another color for low asset-building areas. Keep track of the things that youth say indicate low asset-building potential. Be sure not to focus just on financial factors.

Afterward discuss why some areas of your community have more potential for building assets than others. Brainstorm simple ways your group could help promote more assets in areas that are lacking.

## Building Assets in Other Youth

<u>Focus:</u> **Youth develop a small asset-building program.**

**You will need:**

- chalkboard and chalk

or

- newsprint and a marker

As a group, brainstorm simple ways to build assets in youth in your school, organization, or community. For example, youth may decide to focus on a specific asset type (such as support) and do some of the activities in this book (activities #16 through #33) or create their own activity. Or they may create asset posters to hang around your school, organization, or community. Or they may make bookmarks focusing on some of the assets and distribute them through the school and community libraries. Or they may create a mentoring program where younger youth are paired with older youth. Or they may form a committee to work with the student council, your community's continuing education, or the decision-making board of an organization to suggest ways to build assets in young people.

After you brainstorm a list of at least 10 ideas, choose one to implement. Focus on making your idea simple and doable. (You can always do more later if the first idea goes well. The purpose is for youth to succeed and not get overwhelmed in the process.) Then create a timeline, a plan, and have young people work together to transform the idea into reality.

After you do the activity, discuss what went well and what didn't. Identify ways to make your next try more successful.

## Success at Work

**Focus:** Youth interview a community leader about her or his assets.

*You will need:*
• transportation for your group

As a group, brainstorm leaders in your community whom youth think are successful. Have youth contact two or three of these leaders to see who would be open to a 20-minute conversation with the group at her or his work or volunteer site. Before you go, have youth choose 10 questions about the person's assets that they would like to ask. For example:

• What was your family life like when you were growing up?

• How hard did you work in school? Why? How important do you think school is now?

• What three things were key in helping you be successful?

• What are some values that are important to you? Why?

• What are your strongest skills? Which ones are most challenging for you? Why?

• How much do you have to continue to work at being successful now that you've achieved it?

After the interview talk together as a group about the following kinds of questions:

• What were the major points this leader made when talking about her or his own assets?

• What surprised you most about what this leader said?

• How are this leader's experiences with assets similar to and different from your own experiences with assets?

• What can we learn from this leader about nurturing important assets in our own lives?

## Give and Take

**Focus:** Youth do a service project and think about how helping others builds their own assets.

*You will need:*
• transportation for your group

As a group, choose a service project to do together that involves direct service to people. For example, youth might choose to visit and play games with nursing home residents for a couple of hours or serve people a meal at a soup kitchen. After the group has completed the project, ask youth questions such as these:

• What were some of your strongest impressions about the people we helped?

• Which assets did you observe in the people we were helping?

• Which assets did they seem to be lacking? Why do you think this was so?

• Which of your own assets got a boost from doing this project? Why?

• When you give to others, what do you receive in return?

# PART 2

# External Assets

# Chapter 3

# Support

To grow up healthy, young people need support, love, and encouragement from caring, principled adults. They need homes, schools, congregations, and communities that are accepting, affirming, and safe. Search Institute has identified six "support" assets. This chapter presents activities for helping youth understand the importance of having and giving support, and ways they can build it for themselves and others.

# Family Support

**Family life provides high levels of love and support.**
**64% of youth surveyed have this asset in their lives.**

## Wall of Support

**Focus: Youth identify all the ways their families support them.**

**You will need:**
- a large sheet of newsprint or other type of paper
- markers, paint, or other colorful drawing supplies
- masking tape

Hang a large piece of newsprint or other type of paper on the wall. Title it "Ways Our Families Support Us." Have youth think of all the ways their family members show them love and support. As they think of ideas, have them write or draw pictures of the ideas on the paper. Encourage them to be creative and make the paper look like a graffiti wall. Afterward, ask:

- What are the most common ways our families show their support? What are some unusual ways?

- What were some times in your life when these kinds of support were particularly important? How did they make a difference?

- Some people don't experience as much support as others. How can young people encourage their families to provide more support? (Note to facilitators: Be aware that for some young people, asking for more support from their families is not an option. Help these young people think of other ways to find support.)

- If families have a hard time offering support, how can youth help one another?

### Optional

If several groups are doing this activity at the same time, consider hanging all the sheets of paper together in a long hallway, cafeteria, or other common space for youth and adults throughout the building to see.

## Classroom Census

**Focus: Youth explore the support they experience in their families.**

**You will need:**
- 10 jars
- 10 small squares of green paper for each youth
- 10 small squares of red paper for each youth
- newsprint
- a marker

Label 10 jars: 1. Mother love; 2. Father love; 3. Sibling love; 4. Overall family support; 5. Friendly place; 6. Time together; 7. Tough times; 8. Important issues; 9. Future goals support; and 10. Important in family. Give each youth 10 green squares of paper (about 2" x 2") and 10 red ones. Write these questions on newsprint:

1. Overall, do you feel loved by your mom?
2. Overall, do you feel loved by your dad?
3. Overall, do you feel loved by your siblings?
4. Overall, do you feel supported by your family?
5. Is your home a warm, friendly place to be?
6. Do you like spending time with your family?
7. Do you feel your family usually supports you when you are having a tough time?
8. Do you feel comfortable talking with your parents about issues that are important to you?
9. Do your parents support your future goals?
10. Do you feel like an important part of your family?

Ask youth to put a green paper in the appropriate jar if their answer to the question is "yes" and a red piece if their answer is "no." If youth do not have any siblings, have them skip question #3. If youth live with only one parent, or live with someone other than a parent, encourage them to think of a person who is most like a parent to them.

When everyone has finished, form 10 teams and have each team tally the results from one container and tell the group the total. Ask:

- What are areas where we're most likely to experience support? Why do you think that is?

- Where do we experience less support? Why?

- Did our findings surprise you? Why or why not?

- What advice would you give to youth who don't experience a lot of support in their families?

**#18**

## The Ups and Downs of Support

Think of three times when you felt supported by your family and three times when you didn't. Write about those experiences and how you felt at the time. Then identify other people who could support you during similar times if they happen in the future.

### Felt Supported

What happened: _____

How you felt: _____

Who could give additional support? _____

What happened: _____

How you felt: _____

Who could give additional support? _____

What happened: _____

How you felt: _____

Who could give additional support? _____

### Didn't Feel Supported

What happened: _____

How you felt: _____

Who could you go to for support instead? _____

What happened: _____

How you felt: _____

Who could you go to for support instead? _____

What happened: _____

How you felt: _____

Who could you go to for support instead? _____

# Positive Family Communication

**Young person and her or his parent(s) communicate positively, and young person is willing to seek parent(s') advice and counsel.**

**26% of youth surveyed have this asset in their lives.**

## A Letter to Mom and Dad

**Focus: Youth write a letter to tell their parents about a topic that's difficult to bring up.**

**You will need:**
- writing paper for each youth
- an envelope for each youth

Give each youth a piece of writing paper and an envelope. Encourage youth to write a letter to their parent(s) about a topic that they really want to talk about but have never felt comfortable bringing up. Tell youth that they can decide whether or not to give the letter to their parents, or to show it to anyone. What's most important is to be really honest.

Once youth finish, ask:

- **How did it feel to write about this topic in a letter?**
- **What do you think would happen if you gave your letter to your parent(s)?**
- **What's the worst reaction you might get?**
- **What's the best reaction you might get?**
- **What are other ways you can bring up difficult topics with your parent(s) besides writing a letter?**

### Note

Make it clear that youth do not have to give the letter to their parents. If they choose not to, they might find it useful to think about other ways to bring up tough topics.

## The Family History of Talk

**Focus: Youth talk with their parents about their parents' experiences as a teenager.**

Have youth talk to their parents about their parents' growing-up years. Encourage youth to ask a lot of questions to find out how their parents' family dynamics were similar to and different from the youth's family dynamics. They might ask questions such as:

- **What did you think of your parent(s) when you were a teenager?**
- **What are some of your best memories of your parent(s) when you were a teenager?**
- **What kinds of things did you most often talk about in your family?**
- **Which topics were hard to talk about with your parent(s)? Why?**
- **Who did most of the disciplining?**
- **Who did most of the household chores?**
- **How many hours a week did your parent(s) work outside of the home?**
- **What did you think about your parents' job(s)?**
- **What did you like best about your family? Why?**
- **What did you like least ? Why?**
- **Which rituals or traditions (such as always eating one meal together a day) did your family have that you really liked? Why?**
- **What do you think of the way your parent(s) raised you now that you're a parent yourself?**

Have youth report back what they found. Talk about similarities and differences. Ask:

- **What was it like to ask your parents these kinds of questions?**
- **Which questions got the longest answers? The shortest?**
- **What surprised you the most?**
- **How similar to or different from your lives were your parents' childhood and teenage years?**
- **What can we learn from this experience about how to communicate with and relate to our parents?**

**#21**

## Conversation Topics

Talking with parents is important. In caring families, family members should be able to talk about almost anything. Still, even in the most caring families, some topics will be more difficult to discuss than others.

At the bottom of this page is a list of words. Place those words in the chart below under the category of "easy to talk about" or "difficult to talk about" according to your family dynamics. Once you finish, look at your two lists. Overall, do you feel good about the number of topics you can easily talk about in your family? How can you raise difficult issues?

**Easy to Talk About in My Family**

**Difficult to Talk About in My Family**

| | | | |
|---|---|---|---|
| money | extracurricular activities | parties | fashion |
| friends | conflict | smoking | accessories |
| dating | the state of your room | movies | crime |
| career | time spent as family | politics | race relations |
| future plans | television use | music | religion |
| sex | peer pressure | staying home alone | grades |
| drugs | hopes and dreams | homework | telephone use |
| mistakes | curfews | household chores | privacy |
| accidents | family tension | favors | |
| the family car | | time stress | |

# Other Adult Relationships

**Young person receives support from three or more nonparent adults.**
**41% of youth surveyed have this asset in their lives.**

## Whom Do You Go To?

**Focus:** Youth identify whom they'd turn to for advice in a variety of situations.

**#22**

**You will need:**
- seven sheets of newsprint
- a marker

**M**ake seven newsprint signs. Label them "Neighbor," "Boss," "Activity Director or Coach," "Extended Family," "Teacher," "Other Adult," and "No Other Adult." Space them around the room. Then have youth stand in the middle.

Explain that you're going to name different situations, and youth should run to the sign that reflects who they'd go to for advice on that issue. Explain that extended family could mean any adult in the extended family: grandparents, uncles, aunts, adult cousins, or other relative. Tell youth to choose "other adult" for the other adults and to choose "no other adult" when they feel they wouldn't go to anyone listed.

Name issues or situations such as these, allowing time for youth to run to the appropriate sign each time:
- Just to talk
- To talk about dating and relationships
- What to do after graduation
- Getting into trouble with the police
- If you or a friend got pregnant or got someone pregnant
- Just to hang out with
- Borrowing money
- Questions about alcohol or other drugs
- Getting a bad grade
- Figuring out where you stand on an issue
  Once you finish, ask:
- **Which adults outside of your family do you go to most often for advice and support? Why? Least often? Why?**
- **What keeps you from going to some people?**
- **How do you feel about the number of adult supports you have outside of your family?**
- **Who else can you think of who could give you support?**

## Who Supports You?

**Focus:** Youth think of all the different types of adults they can go to for support.

**#23**

**You will need:**
- chalkboard and chalk
  or
- newsprint and a marker

**H**ave youth brainstorm types of adults (other than parents) who are good to go to for advice and support. Encourage youth to think of adults they usually go to as well as other adults they have never gone to, but could. For example, youth might name a neighbor, a mentor, a boss, a coach, an uncle, a religious youth worker, a teacher, an older sister, and so on. Record all their ideas on newsprint or a chalkboard. Don't discard or evaluate any of their ideas.

When you finish the list, note how many different types of adults can provide support. Then create another list. Have youth brainstorm qualities that make these people good sources of advice and support. For example, youth might list qualities such as patience, understanding, good eye contact, nonjudgmental, sense of humor, and good listening skills. Then ask:
- **What difference does it make for you to have an adult like this in your life?**
- **How would you tell a friend to go about finding a caring adult friend if he or she didn't have one to turn to?**
- **Name one adult, other than your parent(s), whom you would like to get to know better? Why did you choose that person?**
- **How can you go out of your way to see that person this week?**

**EXTERNAL ASSETS: SUPPORT**

## The Adults Around You

**Think about the adults in your life other than your parents. In the space below, write your name in the middle circle. Then write the names of the adults that you know and trust in the surrounding circles, with one name in each circle. If you want to include more than eight adults, draw more circles and add those names. After you finish, star the adult or adults you feel closest to.**

**Then choose one of the people you would like to get to know better and decorate that circle so that it stands out from the others. In the next two weeks do one thing to let that person know he or she is important to you. Consider calling the person on the phone, paying a visit, or sending a letter or E-mail message.**

**You might want to consider choosing a different adult to reach out to each month.**

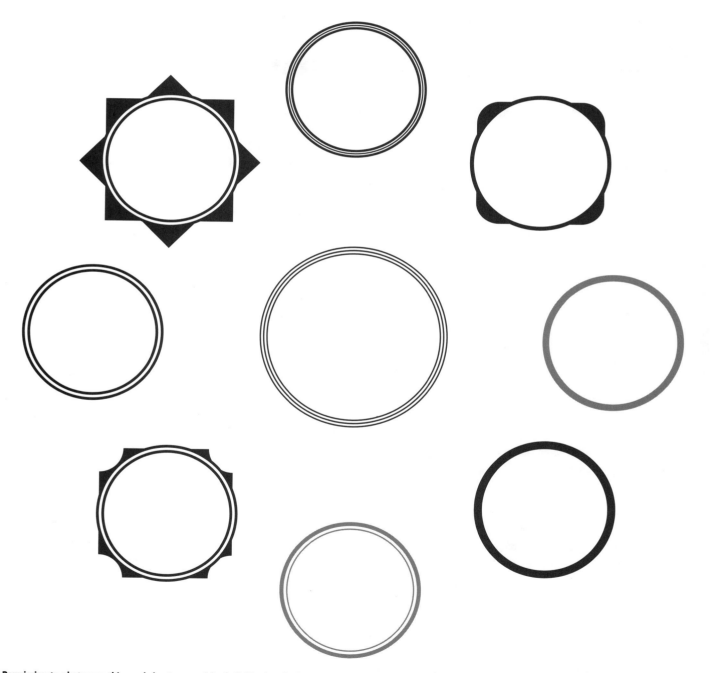

# Caring Neighborhood

### Young person experiences caring neighbors.
### 40% of youth surveyed have this asset in their lives.

## Important Contact

**Focus: Youth initiate a conversation with an adult neighbor after deciding what to talk about with that person.**

**You will need:**
- **writing paper for each youth**
- **pen or pencils— one for each youth**

**H**ave youth each identify one adult neighbor they would like to call or visit within the next few days. Explain that after making contact with that person, each youth will report back to the group on how it went.

Tell youth that the purpose of this contact is to build two-way communication. Ask each youth to list four or five questions they would like to ask this neighbor. Have them work in pairs so they can help each other create their lists, although encourage youth to make their lists based on what they know about this neighbor. For example, youth might ask: I know you like woodworking. What projects have you been working on lately? What did you think of the way the Knicks played yesterday?

Then have youth find a different partner and identify two things happening in their own lives that they could talk about with this neighbor. For example, youth might list: school, work, band, the novel they're reading, and sports.

Tell youth that even if the neighbor doesn't ask questions, they must tell about those two things. Then have youth make their contacts.

**After youth report on their experiences, ask:**

- **What did you do? Describe the experience.**
- **What did you learn?**
- **Did the neighbor ask you many questions? How did that make you feel?**
- **How did the neighbor respond when you told about what was happening with you?**
- **How did that response make you feel?**
- **Were you surprised by anything that happened during your conversation?**
- **Do you want to have another conversation with this neighbor? Why or why not?**
- **Who else could you do this activity with?**

## Communication Roll

**Focus: Youth and adults talk about their life experiences.**

**You will need:**
- **a group of adults to meet with**
- **dice—one for each group of youth and adults**
- **chalkboard and chalk or**
- **newsprint and a marker**

**F**ind a group of nearby adults (who are your neighbors in some way) whom your group could visit or who could visit your group. Consider a senior citizens group, a neighborhood group, a civic group, or school volunteers. Make sure there are about the same number of adults and youth. Make sure you set up ground rules such as listening to one another, respecting people's right not to be pressured to share information, and giving everyone a chance to speak.

Have the two groups form smaller teams of two youth and two adults. Give each team a die. On a chalkboard or newsprint, write this code:

| | |
|---|---|
| 1=school | 4=family |
| 2=work | 5=values |
| 3=friendships and dating | 6=dreams and goals |

(Or choose other categories that fit the two groups.) Then have each person on each team take turns rolling the die. When a number pops up, the person who rolled the die must tell something that has happened to her or him in that area. For example, an adult who rolls the number three may tell about being stood up on a date when he was a teenager and how he felt about it.

Give the teams lots of time to talk. Watch to see what types of relationships start to form. After the meeting, ask youth to talk about their experience. Discuss similarities and differences in the examples adults gave and examples youth gave. Ask them if they felt comfortable in their teams and why or why not.

## Draw Your Neighborhood

In the space below, draw your neighborhood. Make a box to represent each household. If you live in a house, draw the houses on your block. If you live in an apartment building, draw the apartments on your floor or in your building.

After you finish drawing the layout of your neighborhood, write the names of people and pets who live in those homes. If you're not sure of names, describe what you know about the occupants. For example, you might write that you know a man, a woman, a teenage girl, and a black dog live two doors down. If you're not sure who lives there but have a guess about the occupant, write that too.

Analyze your completed picture. How many neighbors do you really know? What do you think your neighbors know about you? How do you feel about your neighbors? Which neighbors seem friendly? Which seem scary? How could you get to know more about your neighbors?

# Caring School Climate

**School provides a caring, encouraging environment.**
**24% of youth surveyed have this asset in their lives.**

## School Pride

<u>Focus:</u> **Youth pinpoint places where they feel cared for within their school(s).**

### #28

*You will need:*
- **a large sheet of newsprint or other type of paper**
- **markers**
- **stick pins of different colors**

**H**ave youth work together to create a large map of their school on the paper. (If your group includes youth from many schools, have them get into teams by school and each create their own map.) Once they finish, hang the map(s) on a bulletin board. Give youth markers and stick pins to label spots on the map that represent places where they feel cared for in their school. For example, a youth might mark the auditorium if he or she feels cared about while doing theater productions there. A basketball player might label the basketball court. Another youth may highlight a history room because of a caring history teacher.

Once youth finish, have them talk about their experiences of a caring school climate. Then ask:

- **What areas in the school(s) seem to reflect the most care? The least?**
- **How do you feel about what you labeled? Do you think, overall, your school(s) is a caring place? Why or why not?**
- **Do you think your school is equally caring of all students? If not, why not?**
- **What things are important for creating a caring climate in school?**
- **What things get in the way of creating a caring climate?**
- **What can you do to help create a more caring school climate?**

## School Census

<u>Focus:</u> **Youth conduct a survey on school climate.**

### #29

*You will need:*
- **access to a copy machine**
- **plenty of sheets of paper**

**H**ave youth conduct a survey of students in their school about school climate. (First have youth get approval to do a survey.) Have youth agree on 20 questions to include. Explain how multiple-choice questions are easier to tabulate and to convince other youth to answer than open-ended questions.

Encourage youth to think of questions that measure students' opinions about school climate. For example, youth may ask:

- **How caring and encouraging do you think our school is?**
  ❏ Very caring  ❏ Somewhat caring  ❏ Not caring at all
- **What do you like best about our school?**
  ❏ Open lunches  ❏ State basketball champions
  ❏ Most youth graduate  ❏ Study hall
  ❏ Other _____
- **What do you like least about our school?**
  ❏ Too many suspensions  ❏ Graffiti on the walls
  ❏ Poor selection in candy machines
  ❏ Not enough class choices  ❏ Other _____
- **Who tends to show a lot of care toward students? (Check all that apply.)**
  ❏ Teachers  ❏ Coaches  ❏ Administrators
  ❏ Paraprofessionals  ❏ Extracurricular adult leaders
  ❏ Other students  ❏ Custodians  ❏ Other _____

After choosing the 20 questions, have the group create and duplicate the survey. Distribute and decide on a plan to collect the surveys and get them tabulated. Ask for volunteers to copy results from each survey onto one master copy. Then ask one or two youth to calculate totals and percentages for each question.

Talk about how to distribute the findings.

## School Wish List

In each of the areas below, write two ideas of what would help make your school a national model of a caring, encouraging school environment.

 **Relationships among students**

1.

2.

 **Extracurricular activities**

1.

2.

 **Student-teacher relationships**

1.

2.

 **Administration**

1.

2.

 **School environment/building**

1.

2.

 **Student government/student council**

1.

2.

 **School social functions**

1.

2.

# Parent Involvement in Schooling

**Parent(s) are actively involved in helping young person succeed in school.
29% of youth surveyed have this asset in their lives.**

## Talk Show Debate

<u>Focus:</u> **Youth debate the pros and cons of parent involvement in school.**

Ask one youth to be a talk show host like a current popular one. Then ask three other youth to serve as guests on the talk show. The rest of the group can be the audience.

Explain that the topic of the show is the controversy about parents being involved in their children's school. Assign each of the youth one of these roles:

• One strongly favors parents being involved in school. This person is on the school board, and he or she has been able to introduce some major changes.

• One strongly opposes any parental involvement. This person works two jobs and says he or she pays a lot of taxes for schools to do their jobs.

• One isn't sure but likes to ask a lot of questions and makes points for both sides.

Start the talk show. Encourage the host to "dig for dirt" from the three youth who are serving as guests and to encourage the audience to ask questions and express their opinions. If youth can't think of ways to support their positions, throw out a few ideas to get them going again. (Worksheet #33 may help with ideas.) After the talk show, ask the group:

• **Why do you think only 29% of youth nationally have parents who are involved in their schooling?**

• **In what ways have your own parents been involved in your education (both now and in the past)?**

• **Would you like for more parents to be involved in your school? Why or why not?**

• **What are the biggest benefits of parent involvement? Biggest drawbacks? What can you do to encourage parents to be more involved?**

## Pass and Talk

<u>Focus:</u> **Youth share their experiences of their parents being involved in their education.**

Find six rocks that are about four inches in diameter. Using a thin-tipped permanent marker, write on each rock one of these questions or instructions:

*You will need:*
• **six rocks, each about four inches in diameter**
• **a thin-tipped permanent marker**

• Tell about a time when your parent really helped you with a school project or homework.

• Are your parents more or less involved in your school now compared to the past?

• Tell about a time when a parent really embarrassed you at school.

• What things can parents do to hinder their youths' success?

• How do you feel about your own parents' involvement in school?

• Describe a positive experience of parent involvement in school (yours or others).

Have youth form six teams. (If your group is small, form fewer teams and rotate the unused rocks.) Give one person on each team one rock. Ask the person with the rock to read the question or instruction silently and then responded to it aloud, without saying the question or instruction. The team then must guess what the question is. If no one guesses it correctly, the person passes the rock to her or his right, and the next person reads the question silently and answers aloud. Teams should continue the activity until someone guesses the question correctly.

Once all the teams have finished, have teams switch rocks. Repeat the activity. Continue repeating the activity until all the teams have answered all six questions.

**#33**

## Getting Your Parents Involved

Youth are often busy. Parents are often busy. Teachers are often busy. But it is important for schools and families to connect in order to build assets—despite their sometimes hectic schedules.

   Think about your parent's schedule. Then check the ways that you think your mom or dad could be involved in your school.

   After you finish filling out the worksheet, show it to your mom or dad. Ask her or him to complete it as well. Then compare your answers. Talk with your parent about ways to increase her or his involvement in your schooling.

| Good Ways for Parents to Get Involved in School: | According to Youth | According to Parent |
|---|---|---|
| 1. Ask youth what happened in school each day. | ❑ | ❑ |
| 2. Set aside time for youth to do homework each day. | ❑ | ❑ |
| 3. Create a space for youth to do homework at home. | ❑ | ❑ |
| 4. Help youth with homework. | ❑ | ❑ |
| 5. Periodically call a teacher to check on how youth is doing. | ❑ | ❑ |
| 6. Participate in a parent-teacher organization. | ❑ | ❑ |
| 7. Attend a school board meeting to see what some of the key issues are. | ❑ | ❑ |
| 8. Go to parent-teacher conferences. | ❑ | ❑ |
| 9. Send a teacher a note of encouragement. | ❑ | ❑ |
| 10. Volunteer to help out at the school. | ❑ | ❑ |
| 11. Other_____. | ❑ | ❑ |

# Chapter 4

# Empowerment

A key developmental need is to be valued
and feel valuable. The empowerment assets
focus on community perceptions of youth and
opportunities for young people to contribute
to society in meaningful ways. Search Institute
has identified four "empowerment" assets.
The activities in this chapter encourage youth
to examine the importance of empowerment
and the places where they feel empowered.

# Community Values Youth

**Young person perceives that adults in the community value youth.**
**20% of youth surveyed have this asset in their lives.**

## Perceptions of Community Perceptions

**Focus:** Youth monitor others in the community to judge perceptions of youth.

Have youth form teams of four (more or less). Have each team create a criteria list of ways to judge public perceptions of youth. Ideas could include adults making eye contact with youth, adults greeting youth, adults smiling at youth, and so on. Encourage youth to make a list of five to six items that would be easily measurable.

Then have each team do a 10-minute monitoring of an area where there are a lot of adults, such as a shopping mall, a fellowship area of a congregation before a religious service, a community event or game, a busy sidewalk, or other high-traffic spot. Afterward ask:

**You will need:**
• writing paper
• pens or pencils

- **Overall, how would you say most of the adults in your study perceived the youth in your group? Why?**
- **What are some of the ways the adults interacted with youth?**
- **What would happen if you were to repeat the activity but make more of an effort to smile, make eye contact, and greet the adults? Why?**
- **Where do you think adults in the community get their ideas about youth? Why?**
- **How do you think that could change? Who has the power to start that change?**

## Community Cafeteria

**Focus:** Youth identify opportunities for involvement in their community.

Explain that one way a community values youth is by offering activities for young people to get involved in. Have youth form eight teams according to types of activities they're most interested in. Possibilities include sports, arts, religious programs, hobbies, social action, service, educational enrichment, and business. (If your group is small, combine or leave out some areas.) Then have each team work together to identify organizations, clubs, and offerings in the community in that area. Youth can find this information through the community newspaper, chamber of commerce, city hall, their school counselor's office, the library, and community education offices.

**You will need:**
• chalkboard and chalk
or
• newsprint and markers

Once teams finish, have them report to the larger group what they found. Write each team's findings on the chalkboard or newsprint. Then ask:

- **What types of activities are most available for youth your age? Where are the gaps?**
- **Were you surprised by what you found?**
- **Overall, by what you see offered to youth, how much do you think the community values youth? Why?**
- **Which community organizations seem to value youth most? Which don't value youth much at all? Why do you think this is so?**

Depending on how much information youth gather, they may want to host an activity fair for other youth to come and learn about opportunities. They could also write an article for their school newspapers.

## The Valuable You

**#36**

Sometimes we may not realize that we're valued by other people. Identify four adults, including your parent(s), an adult relative, and one or two other adults in your life, such as a teacher, coach, boss, youth group leader, neighbor, etc. In the "ribbon" on each of the diamonds below, write the name of one of those people.

Call or visit each of these four people and ask them why they think you're a valuable person in this community. People always know, and what they say may surprise you. After you talk with them, write what each person said in the diamond labeled with their name.

**Asset #8**

# Youth as Resources

**Young people are given useful roles in the community.
24% of youth surveyed have this asset in their lives.**

## Big Brothers, Big Sisters

<u>Focus:</u> **Youth inquire how they can be resources for a mentoring program.**

**#37**

*You will need:*
- **writing paper**
- **pens or pencils**

Tell youth that you're inviting a person from a mentoring organization to talk about how and why the organization matches youth and adults with children. Have youth each write down one question they would like to ask that person. Examples of questions include: What kinds of things do mentors and mentees do together? Who can be a mentor? Who can get a mentor? Why is it important for young people to have mentors?

Collect all the questions and have two or three youth read them aloud. As a group, agree on five questions to ask the person. Ask for five volunteers each to ask one of the questions during the question-and-answer period. Explain that if there is more time, youth can ask other questions after the five have been answered.

Then have a representative from a mentoring program such as One to One or Big Brothers/Big Sisters speak to your group. Have that person explain the importance of pairing youth with children and some of the results of those relationships.

Let youth ask their questions, starting with the five that the group agreed upon. After the person has left, have the group write and send a joint thank-you letter to the speaker in which they name the ways they think her or his work is important.

Encourage youth to consider becoming a mentor for a younger child or to seek an adult mentor for themselves through the organization.

## Activity Proposal

<u>Focus:</u> **Youth develop an idea for a new activity that gives them something useful to do or learn.**

**#38**

*You will need:*
- **writing paper**
- **pens or pencils**

Have youth work together to develop a proposal for one idea for an activity that they would like to see available in their school, community, congregation, or other organization. Youth may wish to develop a new activity that would be worthwhile or consider proposing an idea to make an existing activity more meaningful. Encourage them to think through details such as benefits, timing, number of youth involved, sponsors, funds needed, and so on. As youth develop the proposal, talk about what they hope to accomplish with the activity and how it will help youth grow up healthy and successful.

Once the proposal is fleshed out, have the youth present the proposal to the decision-making body of the organization (such as a principal or student council at a school, a youth group leader or leadership council at a congregation, or the community education committee of a community).

The proposal might generate some good media attention in your community paper. Consider asking youth to write letters to a school or local newspaper explaining their idea.

## #39  Important Roles

**Everybody has a number of roles they play in their life. For example, a person can be a son or daughter, a student, a sibling, a team leader, and so on. Write one important thing you do in each of the designated roles below. For example, in your role as a student you might write that you learn and ask questions; as a family member you participate in family decisions and mow the lawn.**

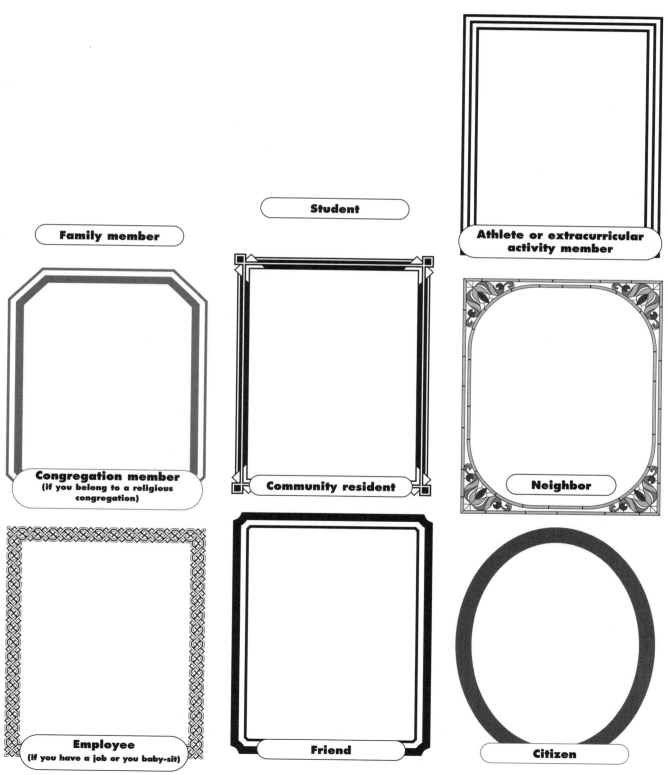

Student

Family member

Athlete or extracurricular activity member

Congregation member
(if you belong to a religious congregation)

Community resident

Neighbor

Employee
(if you have a job or you baby-sit)

Friend

Citizen

# Service to Others

**Young person serves in the community one hour or more per week.**
**50% of youth surveyed have this asset in their lives.**

EXTERNAL ASSETS: EMPOWERMENT

## Penny Power

**Focus:** Youth experience what it's like to give and to receive.

**#40**

**You will need:**
- five pennies for each student

Have youth sit in groups of four or five. Give each youth five pennies. Explain that when you say "go," you want people to hoard their own pennies while trying to get more pennies from the other people in their group.

After a few minutes, stop the activity. Explain that the activity will be repeated except that people are to try to give as many pennies as they can to others in their group without accepting any. Say "go" and watch what happens.

Afterward, ask questions such as these:
- **What was it like to try to take pennies from others? Give them away?**
- **Which part of the activity raised more negative feelings in you? Why?**
- **Which part of the activity raised more positive feelings in you? Why?**
- **Is it important to give and to serve others?**
- **What experience have you had in giving to others (your time, money, talents, other resources)?**

## Random Acts of Service

**Focus:** Youth choose simple ways to serve others.

**#41**

**You will need:**
- chalkboard and chalk or
- newsprint and a marker

Have youth brainstorm a list of simple, easy ways to serve others. Write all the ideas on a chalkboard or newsprint. Examples might include taking out the garbage, shoveling a snowy walk, mowing someone's lawn, returning books to a library, writing a thinking-of-you note to someone, sending a coupon for ice cream or a movie to a child, and so on.

Then have youth each choose one thing they could do within the next week (either anonymously or not). Have youth observe the receiver's reactions and also notice their own reaction to the receiver's reactions.

The next time you meet together, ask questions such as these:
- **What activity did you choose? Why?**
- **How did you feel while you were doing the activity? Why?**
- **How did you feel after completing the activity? Why?**
- **How did the receiver's reaction affect your feelings about service? Why?**
- **Do you want to do other acts of service? Why or why not?**

## A Contract to Serve

**#42**

Choose a kind of service you would like to do (for example, mowing a neighbor's lawn, baby-sitting so the parents can run errands, or cleaning up litter from your block) and how much time you can realistically spend doing it. Then fill in the contract below. Consider showing or giving the contract to the person you plan to help.

# Contract for Service

I, _____ ,
(your name)

make a commitment to

_____ .
(type of service)

This service will be of help to _____
(name of receiver)

because _____ .
(reason for doing the project)

I realistically can spend about _____ hours on this project.

I intend to start by _____ .
(date)

_____    _____
(your signature)                              (today's date)

# Asset #10  Safety

**Young person feels safe at home, at school, and in the neighborhood.**
**55% of youth surveyed have this asset in their lives.**

## Safe—or Not?

**Focus:** Youth take a stand on safety in various aspects of their lives.

### #43

**You will need:**
• a piece of rope or
• masking tape

Before you do this activity, designate one area to be home base. Designate another area as a tightrope area. Either lay a piece of rope on the floor or use masking tape to symbolize a rope.

Have youth all stand. Make sure there is enough room for youth to move from one area to another. Explain that you're going to name various aspects of their lives, one at a time. After each one is named, youth should move either to home base (if they always feel safe in the place you mention) or to the tightrope and try to stand only on the tightrope (if they sometimes or always feel unsafe in the place you mention). Name places one at a time, including their neighborhood, their school, a congregation, a nearby rural community, shops, your state, youth hangouts, a nearby suburb, the United States of America, after-school activities, home, your closest city at 1 a.m. on a weekend, the world. After each named place, give youth time to move to either the home base or the tightrope. Allow youth time to see how their classmates answered.

Afterward, ask questions such as these:
• Where do you feel most safe? Why?
• Where do you feel least safe? Why?
• What makes you feel safe in a certain place? What makes you feel unsafe?
• What suggestions do you have to make some of the unsafe places in your life more safe?

## Safety in Numbers

**Focus:** Youth name characteristics of safe communities.

### #44

**You will need:**
• writing paper
• pens or pencils— one for each group
• chalkboard and chalk or
• newsprint and a marker

Form three or four teams each with about the same number of members. Give each team a piece of paper and something with which to write. Explain that the teams are going to compete against each other. Each team will have five minutes to identify as many different aspects of safe communities as they can think of (for example, people you trust, areas you can go to if you need help or feel threatened).

Give teams time to do the activity. After five minutes, have teams count up the number of safety characteristics they identified. Then together, create one long list from the four groups and put all the items on a chalkboard or newsprint.

Then ask the whole group questions such as:
• How easy was it to think of different characteristics of safe communities? Why?
• After naming all these aspects of safe communities, does it make you feel more safe or more unsafe in your community? Why?
• What can we do to make our community more safe?

## Top Five

**What are your biggest concerns about safety right now? List the five biggest worries you have about safety. Write them in order of priority.**

## 1.

## 2.

## 3.

## 4.

## 5.

**Now list five things that help you feel safe.**

## 1.

## 2.

## 3.

## 4.

## 5.

**During the next two weeks, pay attention to how often you feel really safe and how often you feel unsafe. Are you more likely to feel safe or unsafe? What are some things you can do to make sure you usually feel safe?**

# Chapter 5

# Boundaries and Expectations

Not only do young people need support, they also need boundaries and expectations that guide them to make positive choices. These boundaries and expectations are put in place by families, schools, neighborhoods, adults, and peers. In addition, these same people and social structures send messages about what they expect of young people—whether the messages are intentional or not. Search Institute identifies six "boundaries and expectations assets." The activities in this chapter help youth understand and appreciate the importance of these assets and explore ideas for working with parents on building these assets in their lives.

# Family Boundaries

**Family has clear rules and consequences, and monitors the young person's whereabouts. 43% of youth surveyed have this asset in their lives.**

## Can of Worms

**Focus: Youth compare parents' standards on a variety of issues.**

**You will need:**

- four empty one-pound cans (such as coffee cans)
- several sheets of white paper
- scissors
- access to a copy machine

Bring four empty one-pound cans to the group. On a piece of paper write these items (or others more appropriate for your group): clothing, weekend curfew, weekday curfew, use of the car, dating, part-time work, extracurricular activities, friends, homework, asking for something, mealtime etiquette, expressing anger, expressing sadness, celebrating, drinking alcohol, and TV viewing.

Make three photocopies of this paper. Then cut each paper into strips so that each strip has a different item. Put all the strips from one paper into one can, and do the same with the other papers and cans.

Have youth form four teams. Give each team a can. Have youth take turns picking one piece of paper at a time out of the can and reading it aloud. Then ask the youth to tell what boundaries her or his parent(s) have for that item. (If parents haven't set boundaries on that topic, youth may say what they think their parents would want them to do!) The youth keeps her or his strip of paper and gives the can to the person on her or his left. That person repeats the activity. Continue until all the strips of paper are drawn. Then have youth repeat the activity. Then ask:

- **What common boundaries do parents set for youth?**
- **Do most parents set reasonable boundaries? Too strict? Too lenient? Why do you think that is?**
- **How do your parents decide on their boundaries (e.g., personal experience, talk with you about them, what they think is "right," religious beliefs)?**
- **How would your life be better or worse if your parent(s) didn't set boundaries?**
- **What would you tell a friend who had major disagreements with a parent about boundaries?**

## Evolving Role Play

**Focus: Youth role-play the effects of three different parenting styles.**

**You will need:**

- 3 x 5 note cards—at least one per youth

Ask three youth to be volunteers. Have one pretend to be a teenager whose parents need to know every detail about where the teenager goes, what he or she does, and with whom he or she spends time. Have another volunteer be a teenager who has parents who seem not to care about these things. The third volunteer should pretend to be a teenager who has parents who want to know what the teenager does but aren't overly protective.

Give each of the other youth one 3 x 5 card. Explain that youth who are watching the role play can give one of the players an idea of things to do during the role play that would fit their assigned role. For example, a youth might slip a note that says, "act really defensive" to the volunteer who has overprotective parents or "brag about your freedom" to the volunteer whose parents don't seem to care.

Have the volunteers begin by acting out a scene such as this: Three friends get together on a week night to have some ice cream. The friend with the permissive parents wants the other two to go to an 11 p.m. movie with her or him. Or brainstorm other scenes.

Then have the role play begin. Encourage youth to give the volunteers ideas throughout the role play. Afterward, ask:

- **Which of the three characters could you most identify with? Why?**
- **What are the advantages of each of the teenagers' situations? The disadvantages?**
- **What are ways that each of these characters could improve her or his situation?**
- **Is it important for parents to know where their teenagers are, what they are doing, and who they are with? Why?**

## #48 At Which Age?

**If you were the parent, at what age would you allow your child—if ever—to do the following activities?**

| | Age | Why That Age? |
|---|---|---|
| 1. Wear makeup | _____ | _____ |
| 2. Have a credit card | _____ | _____ |
| 3. Work part time during the school year | _____ | _____ |
| 4. Drink alcohol for the first time | _____ | _____ |
| 5. Get her or his ears pierced | _____ | _____ |
| 6. Buy a car | _____ | _____ |
| 7. Go on a group date | _____ | _____ |
| 8. Go on an individual date | _____ | _____ |
| 9. Go steady (date someone exclusively) | _____ | _____ |
| 10. Stay out until midnight on weekends | _____ | _____ |
| 11. Not have a curfew | _____ | _____ |
| 12. Rent a hotel room | _____ | _____ |
| 13. Have a boy/girl party | _____ | _____ |
| 14. Open a checking account | _____ | _____ |
| 15. Choose her or his own clothes | _____ | _____ |
| 16. Stay home alone when parents go out of town | _____ | _____ |
| 17. Cook an entire family meal | _____ | _____ |
| 18. Take a weekend camping trip with peers | _____ | _____ |
| 19. Go to an R-rated movie | _____ | _____ |
| 20. Go out of state with a friend's family | _____ | _____ |

# School Boundaries

**School provides clear rules and consequences.**
**46% of youth surveyed have this asset in their lives.**

## "If I Set the School Rules!"

**Focus:** Youth brainstorm appropriate school boundaries.

**#49**

**You will need:**
- chalkboard and chalk or
- newsprint and a marker

Ask for a volunteer to take notes on a chalkboard. Have the group brainstorm a list of school boundaries to discuss. For example, the group might mention boundaries such as the number of sick days allowed per semester, rules about skipping class, and homework expectations. Then have the group brainstorm "ideal" limits or guidelines for each boundary, which the volunteer writes on the board. Then brainstorm consequences for violating those limits. Have the group work together to come to a consensus of what would be realistic, fair, and acceptable to students, teachers, and school administrators.

After youth finish discussing one boundary, have them work on three or four more. Then brainstorm together all the factors that go into setting appropriate boundaries (such as age and previous behavior). If youth wish, they could create a written report to distribute to the student council or school administrator.

Afterward, ask questions such as these:
- **Which school boundaries are you currently most happy with? Why?**
- **Which ones seem most unfair? Why?**
- **What suggestions do you have for making those boundaries more fair?**
- **Are school boundaries important? Why?**

## Unclear Boundaries

**Focus:** Youth experience what it's like when boundaries aren't articulated well.

**#50**

**You will need:**
- 150 toothpicks
- 150 gumdrops
- a chalkboard and chalk or
- newsprint and markers

Form three groups of about equal players. Make lots of room since the teams will be working independently of each other and should not be able to see what the other teams are doing. Hand out about 50 toothpicks and about 50 gumdrops to each group. With one group, whisper (so that the other groups do not hear) that the members of this group can eat as many gumdrops as they wish but to do so discreetly and quietly so that the other groups don't notice. Explain that they can stick as many toothpicks as they wish into each gumdrop used.

Write these instructions on a chalkboard or newsprint: "Build a structure using the toothpicks and the gumdrops. The goal is to be the first group to finish, but all of the toothpicks and gumdrops must be used." Then have the groups begin. Once a group wins, stop the activity. Have the groups examine the winning structure. Then gather everyone together and discuss questions such as these:
- **How do you feel about the structure that the winning team made? Why?**
- **Did the winning team follow the boundaries given? Why or why not?**
- **Was the game set up fairly?**
- **What would have happened if every group had been told the same boundaries?**
- **What experiences have you had when boundaries weren't well articulated or were confusing?**
- **Why do you think boundaries aren't always clear?**

## Ideal School Boundaries

**#51**

Imagine yourself as the one who makes all the final decisions about boundaries at your school. Write what you think would be a fair and clear boundary for each of the areas below.

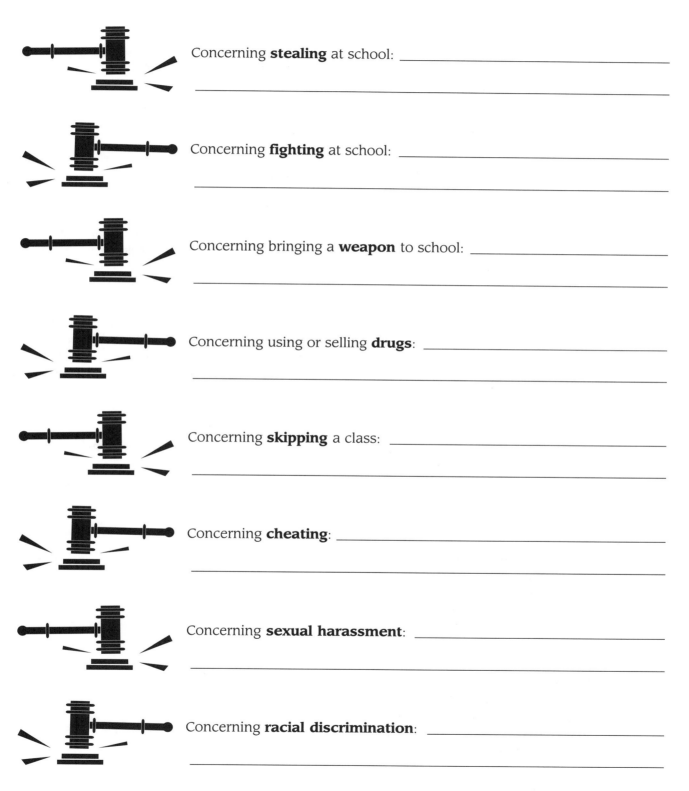

Concerning **stealing** at school: _____

_____

Concerning **fighting** at school: _____

_____

Concerning bringing a **weapon** to school: _____

_____

Concerning using or selling **drugs**: _____

_____

Concerning **skipping** a class: _____

_____

Concerning **cheating**: _____

_____

Concerning **sexual harassment**: _____

_____

Concerning **racial discrimination**: _____

_____

# Neighborhood Boundaries

**Neighbors take responsibility for monitoring young people's behaviors.**

**46% of youth surveyed have this asset in their lives.**

## How Would You Respond?

<u>Focus:</u> **Youth role-play reactions to various behaviors of neighbors.**

**#52**

**You will need:**
- **three index cards for each youth**

Give each person three index cards. Have each person write one major neighborhood offense, one minor neighborhood offense, and a third neighborhood offense of their choosing—one offense on each card.

Then have youth mill around the room. When you yell "find a neighbor," each person should pair up with one nearby person. (If you have an extra person, have a threesome form.) Have each pair take turns reading their offenses one at a time, allowing the partner to respond with what he or she thinks would be an appropriate neighborly response. Give partners time to go through each of their cards, taking turns.

Once partners finish, have youth mingle around the room again until you yell "find a neighbor!" Youth should then pair up with someone nearby, with whom they haven't previously been paired.

Repeat the activity three or four times. Then bring the youth together to discuss questions such as these:

- **What were some of the major offenses people thought of? What were some of the minor offenses?**
- **How did it feel to respond to the situations you were given? Why?**
- **Is it easy to be a neighbor? Why or why not?**
- **How would most of your neighbors respond to some of the situations you presented today?**
- **How do you feel about the boundaries in your neighborhood? Why?**
- **How can we have better neighborhood boundaries?**

## The Ideal Neighborhood

<u>Focus:</u> **Youth think about the types of activities for teens in a "perfect" neighborhood.**

**#53**

**You will need:**
- **large sheets of paper—one for each group**
- **markers, crayons, or other drawing tools**

Have youth form teams of four (more or less). Give each team a large sheet of paper to draw a perfect neighborhood that is ideal for people of all ages. Encourage youth to talk about problems and challenges that currently exist in their own neighborhoods that keep them from becoming like the utopian neighborhood they've drawn.

Then have each team show their drawing to the rest of the group while suggesting one or two ideas for how their neighborhood could become more like their picture. Then ask:

- **What are the most important things to have in an ideal neighborhood?**
- **Which of these things are available in our/your neighborhood? Why?**
- **Where are the biggest gaps in our/your neighborhood?**
- **What things can youth do to make their neighborhoods better places to live?**

## Neighbors Who Keep a Close Eye

**Think about the ideal characteristics of a caring neighbor who keeps an eye out for children and youth. How would they act? What would they say?**

**Write characteristics of a caring neighbor in the lens portion of the glasses below. List as many characteristics as you can think of.**

# Adult Role Models

**Parent(s) and other adults model positive, responsible behavior.**
**27% of youth surveyed have this asset in their lives.**

## Following the Leader

**Focus:** Youth follow various ways of modeling.

**#55**

**F**orm a large circle. Explain that you want youth to follow your verbal instructions, not your actions. Tell youth to jump up and down while you sit down. Then have youth run in place while you walk slowly from one part of the circle to the other. Have youth yawn while you smile and wink at them.

Stop the action. Explain that you now want youth to follow your actions, not your words. Start turning around in place while saying, "Don't turn around." Then hop on one foot while saying, "No hopping, only sitting is allowed." Then start yelling, "Don't yell anymore. Just whisper! Do you hear me! Whisper! Whisper! Whisper!"

Stop the action. Explain that you want youth to follow your instructions. Have youth march while you march. Then have youth sit down as you sit down. Then have youth hold hands in the circle as you hold your neighbor's hand.

Then ask questions such as these:

• How did it feel to follow my verbal instructions when my actions were doing something else? Why?

• How did it feel to follow my actions when my words contradicted what I was doing? Why?

• Was it more difficult to follow the verbal instructions with contradictory actions or the actions with the contradictory words? Why?

• Why is it important for role models and leaders to do what they want others to do?

## Celebrities and Newsmakers

**Focus:** Youth identify positive and negative celebrity and "newsmaker" role models.

**#56**

*You will need:*

• **two sheets of newsprint**

• **a selection of current teen, sport, and news-magazines**

• **scissors**

• **tape or glue**

**H**ang two pieces of newsprint, one on each wall. Write "Positive Role Models" at the top of one newsprint. Write "Negative Role Models" at the top of the other. Distribute recent teen, sport, and newsmagazines that youth can cut up.

Ask youth to cut out pictures of celebrities and newsmakers. Ask them to tape or glue the pictures onto the newsprint sheet they feel is appropriate for each picture.

After youth finish, ask questions such as these:

• Who are the people you chose for each category? Describe some of the reasons these people are positive or negative role models.

• How easy or difficult was this activity? Why?

• Do you think some of the same people could appear on both newsprint sheets? Why or why not?

• Why are celebrities and newsmakers important?

• What are some of the dangers in looking up to these people?

• How should we judge whether a celebrity or newsmaker is a worthwhile role model or not?

**#57**

## Role Models in Your Life

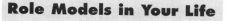

Who are the adult role models in your life? In each of the three gingerbread people outlines below, write the name of someone you look up to. Include an adult family member, a non-family member adult who knows you, and one national or world role model. An adult family member could be a parent, adult sibling, aunt, uncle, grandparent, or adult cousin. A non-family member adult could be a teacher, coach, neighbor, family friend, or some other adult. A national or world role model could be a celebrity, national leader, author, or someone else who has been in the news at some point in their lives.

After you write the name of each person, write what you admire about each person inside of her or his outline.

**Adult family member**

**Non-family member adult**

**National or world role model**

# Positive Peer Influence

**Young person's best friends model responsible behavior.**
**60% of youth surveyed have this asset in their lives.**

**EXTERNAL ASSETS: BOUNDARIES AND EXPECTATIONS**

## Media Review

**Focus:** Youth analyze media messages about friendship.

**#58**

Form seven teams of about the same number of youth. Ask each team to discuss one of these media: videos, current movie releases, broadcast television, cable television, radio, newspapers, and magazines. (If your group is small, form fewer teams and eliminate some of the types of media.) Have team members discuss the messages their designated media gives about having friends who model responsible behavior.

Have each team report on its discussion to the larger group. Then as a group, rank the seven media from the one with the most messages about positive friends to the one with the fewest positive messages about friends.

Ask the following questions:

• What types of messages are most common about friends?

• Are they mostly positive or negative messages?

• Do the media's messages about friends fit with your own experiences? In what ways are they similar and different?

• In what ways have you seen friends being positive influences on others? How can you be a positive influence on your friends?

## Friendship Verse

**Focus:** Youth rewrite lyrics to simple songs to focus on characteristics of positive friends.

**#59**

**You will need:**

• chalkboard and chalk

or

• newsprint and a marker

Have youth form teams of three. Have each team choose one simple tune, such as "Twinkle, Twinkle, Little Star" or "Humpty Dumpty," and write a verse that deals with positive friends. Or they could choose advertising jingles that most youth are familiar with. Then have each team perform the tune for the group. For example, a verse for "Mary Had a Little Lamb" might be: "Friends who care and friends who share / are great friends / are great friends / friends who're there when you feel blue / are the best friends to have."

After all the teams have performed, list all of the characteristics of friends that were included in the songs. Then ask:

• Are these the most important characteristics for friends to have? What other things would you add?

• Why do you think these characteristics are important?

• As you think about your own friends, what are some areas where you see them being positive influences and having these traits?

• How can you be a positive influence on your friends?

**#60**

## Model Photo Album

Choose two friends you really look up to. Place photographs of your two friends in the places designated below. If you don't have a photograph, consider taking one with an instant camera, drawing a picture, or just writing the name of your friend in the picture frame. Under each picture, write which attributes you particularly like and admire about each friend.

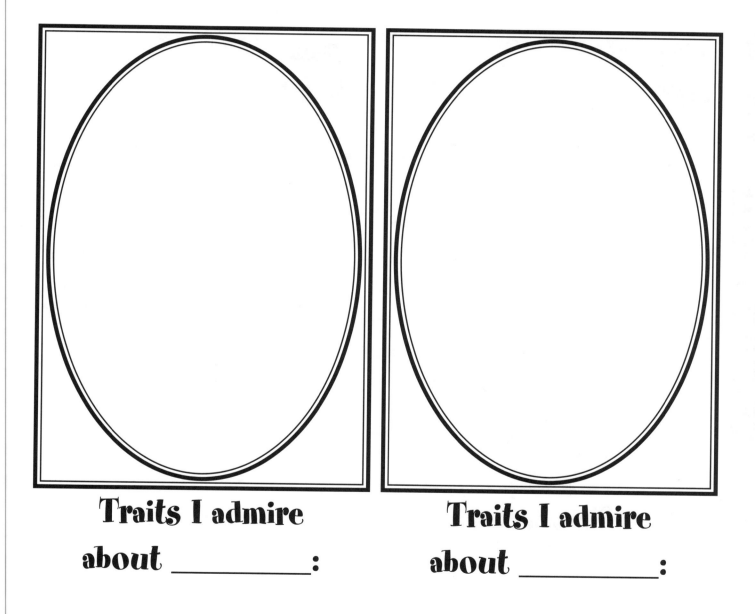

# Traits I admire about _____:

# Traits I admire about _____:

# High Expectations

**Both parent(s) and teachers encourage the young person to do well.**

**41% of youth surveyed have this asset in their lives.**

## Living with Expectations

**Focus:** Youth discuss how they felt in certain situations about people's expectations of them.

**#61**

Have youth each find a partner who is wearing the same color socks that they are wearing. (If you have an extra person, have a threesome form.) Have pairs take turns telling about times when they didn't meet someone's expectations. How did the other people react? How did the youth feel?

After pairs finish, have youth each find a partner who is wearing the same number of rings that they are wearing on both hands. Have pairs take turns discussing this situation: Tell about a time when you exceeded someone's expectations. Then ask them to discuss how they felt and how the other people reacted.

After pairs finish, have youth each find a partner who has the same color hair. Have pairs take turns discussing what they wish others would expect of them and why.

Then bring the group together and discuss questions such as these:

- Overall, do the adults in your lives (teachers, parents, and other adults) expect too much, too little, or just the right amount of you? Why do you feel that way?
- What's difficult about living with people's expectations?
- How can you help the adults in your lives have realistic, challenging, high expectations that are just right for you?

## Inspirational Sayings

**Focus:** Youth critique sayings about expectations.

**#62**

Write the following sayings on a chalkboard or newsprint: "Dream Big," "Expect the Best," "You Can Do More than You Think," "Dream Impossible Dreams—and Do Them," and "Be the Best You Can Be."

*You will need:*
- chalkboard and chalk or
- newsprint and a marker

Have youth form groups of three or four. Explain that groups are to discuss and critique each of the sayings. Have groups discuss questions such as these: Which are realistic? Which are not? What are the problems with any of the sayings? Which are good advice? Why?

Afterward bring everyone together and discuss questions such as these:

- Many people like to collect sayings, phrases, and quotes such as these and others. Why?
- Do you have any favorite sayings of your own?
- Do these sayings inspire you or put too much pressure on you? Why?
- How do others inspire you?
- How do you inspire yourselves?

**#63**

In the talk bubbles below, write one thing each of the people or group of people named expects of you. After you finish, put a star next to those whose expectations and encouragement help you in positive ways.

Parents

Teachers

You

# Chapter 6

# Constructive Use of Time

A key to helping youth thrive is their involvement in constructive, structured activities. The activities challenge and stimulate young people and teach them positive skills, attitudes, and values. Search Institute identifies four "constructive use of time" assets. The activities in this chapter encourage youth to get involved in these positive, asset-building activities.

# Creative Activities

**Young person spends three or more hours per week in lessons or practice in music, theater, or other arts.**

**19% of youth surveyed have this asset in their lives.**

## The Arts Around You

<u>Focus:</u> **Youth identify opportunities for tapping into their artistic interests.**

Have youth choose one form of artistic expression they like best or are most interested in learning about (e.g., music lessons, orchestra, painting, drawing, theater, dance, choir, etc.). Then have youth identify groups, training, or other opportunities within your community or school to learn more about that form of fine art. Encourage youth to find out about the time commitment, the place, the price, and the experience required to be involved.

Have youth report what they find to the group. Then ask:

- **In what ways are you already involved in arts?**
- **What do you get out of your involvement?**
- **Why do you think it's an asset to spend three or more hours each week in music or other arts training or practice?**
- **Which artistic form of expression are you somewhat interested in but have never tried?**
- **Do you think you might try it someday? Why or why not?**

## Artistic Try-On

<u>Focus:</u> **Youth try out different types of art.**

Ask youth about the artistic programs they're involved in. Ask for volunteers to bring in materials from the various arts they are involved in, such as a musical instrument, music to sing, a costume from a play, materials with which to paint or draw, an original poem or story, and so on. Make sure you have a volunteer representing each of the arts areas: instrumental music, vocal music, theater, visual arts, and writing. (Feel free to include other arts such as makeup, clowning, pottery, and others.) Have the volunteers demonstrate their art to the group and then invite other youth who have never tried these types of art to try each one. Typically, youth try different art activities early on in elementary school and rarely get the chance to do so again.

If youth feel self-conscious about being volunteers to demonstrate to the class, invite your school band conductor, choir director, or orchestra conductor for music, an art teacher or artist, a theater teacher, and a writing teacher.

After youth have experimented, ask questions such as these:

- **What is the most rewarding part of being involved in the arts?**
- **As you tried some of these different arts, which ones seemed like they'd be the most fun to learn? Why?**
- **What tips for getting started would you give youth who aren't really into any arts?**
- **Do you think artistic expression is important? Why?**

## Opening Yourself Up to Creativity

**#66**

One of the aspects of strong arts programs is that they open you up to being creative. Teresa Amabile, Ph.D., author of *Growing Up Creative* (Creative Education Foundation, 1989), has identified a number of traits of creative people. Check each of the traits below that you currently have and star the ones you want to work on.

1. ☐ I like to use my imagination.

2. ☐ I like to try new things to develop new interests.

3. ☐ I like to ask a lot of questions.

4. ☐ I express my opinions while respecting others' opinions.

5. ☐ I feel like I have a lot of choices.

6. ☐ I take time each week to daydream and loaf.

7. ☐ I surround myself with people who encourage me to try new things.

8. ☐ I make a lot of decisions for myself.

9. ☐ I consider myself a curious person.

10. ☐ I enjoy playing.

# Youth Programs

**Young person spends three or more hours per week in sports, clubs, or organizations at school and/or in community organizations. 59% of youth surveyed have this asset in their lives.**

## School Activity Hunt

**Focus:** Youth compile a list of available extracurricular activities.

**You will need:**
• access to a copy machine
• copy paper

If your school publishes a directory of all extracurricular activities, photocopy that listing for each youth in the group. (If not, consider having your group put a directory together to distribute to other youth.) If youth in your program are from more than one school, ask them each to try to find a directory for their own school. Have youth read through the list(s) of activities and each identify one that sounds interesting that they have never tried.

Then have youth locate the adviser or the student president of that group and find out more about that group. For example, have youth take notes on the length of time the activity meets, how often it meets, what the requirements for involvement are, and how many youth are involved.

Once youth complete their investigation, compile the findings and create a book for each school involved. Photocopy the book(s) for each youth. Depending on how much youth get into the activity, consider making the book available to other youth in the school(s).

When you near completion of the project, ask:

• What kinds of activities seem most interesting?

• How likely are you to get involved with one or more of these activities? Why or why not?

• Which characteristics of these activities make them beneficial? What are some drawbacks?

• In addition to knowing about available opportunities, what else would make it easier or more likely for you to get involved?

## Involvement in Activities

**Focus:** Youth explain why young people do or don't get involved in youth programs.

**You will need:**
• paper
• a pen or pencil for each group

Form two groups. Give each group a piece of paper and something with which to write. Have one group focus on school activities and the other group work on community activities. Explain that each group is to make a list of the benefits of getting involved in youth programs in their setting and to make a list of why young people don't get involved.

After groups finish, have them read their lists to the entire group. Then discuss questions such as these:

• **Which is it easier for youth to get involved in: school or community activities? Why?**

• **Are there programs in our community that are more popular than others? Why?**

• **Why is it important to get involved in youth programs?**

• **What keeps youth from getting involved?**

• **What are reasons youth do get involved in some programs?**

• **How could we encourage more youth to see the benefits of program involvement?**

**#69**

## Essential Extracurricular Activities

List each extracurricular activity, sport, club, or organization that you're involved with in your school or community. Next to each activity, write the approximate number of hours per week you spend with this organization. (If the activity happens only monthly, divide that time into four to find the weekly total. Or, if you're involved in an activity four times a year, figure out the average number of weekly hours that activity entails.) Then add up the hours at the bottom. How close are you to spending three or more hours a week doing extracurricular activities? In the last column, write ways these activities help you (e.g., make friends, learn skills, plan for a career, stay fit).

Activity Name     Hours Per Week     How It Helps Me

_____   _____   _____

_____   _____   _____

_____   _____   _____

_____   _____   _____

_____   _____   _____

_____   _____   _____

_____   _____   _____

_____   _____   _____

Total Hours Per Week  _____

# Religious Community

**Young person spends one or more hours per week in activities in a religious institution.**

**64% of youth surveyed have this asset in their lives.**

## Role Models

**Focus:** Youth study the religious involvement of their role models.

**#70**

Have youth identify some of their well-known role models. For example, youth may wish to name current or former presidents, music stars, movie stars, Dr. Martin Luther King Jr., sports stars, Gandhi, Mother Teresa, and others.

Form teams of three. Have each team discuss one role model and that person's involvement in religion. (They may need to do some research to learn more about the person.) Have teams discuss questions such as these:

- **Of the role models we've named who have made significant contributions to society, how involved are they in religion? What impact does that involvement seem to have on them?**
- **Does learning about role models' religious involvement change your view of them? Why or why not?**
- **Is religious involvement usually positive or negative? Why?**
- **Is it important to know a person's religious involvement before deciding whether to look up to her or him? Why or why not?**
- **How does religious involvement affect teenagers you know?**
- **How important is religious involvement to you? Why?**

## Yellow Pages Search

**Focus:** Youth identify and learn about available religious youth programs.

**#71**

*You will need:*
- **several community phone books**
- **access to a copy machine**
- **writing paper**
- **pens or pencils**

Form teams of three. Give each threesome the yellow pages of your community phone book. Have the teams look under "Churches," "Synagogues," "Mosques," and "Religious Organizations." Count the entries and divide the entries equally among the teams. Explain that each team is to find out what each of these groups offers youth in the community.

Have teams each contact their assigned organizations and ask questions such as these:

- **Do you have a youth program?**
- **If so, when does it meet? For how long?**
- **Do you have to be a member of the congregation or organization in order to participate?**
- **About how many youth are involved?**
- **What other programs do you have for youth?**
- **Who can give us more information?**
- **Do you have information about your program that you could send us? (If so, please send.)**

Then have the teams compile their information into a report. Combine all the reports together into one large report and make copies for each youth. Talk about these kinds of questions:

- **What kinds of programs are most common in religious organizations? What are some unique programs?**
- **What features of programs you learned about are most interesting to you? What features are "turnoffs"?**
- **If you could make three recommendations to religious youth program leaders, what would you say?**

## What About Your Involvement?

**#72**

**Think about the positive and negative experiences you've had in a religious organization. Briefly write about one negative experience and one positive experience. Then write about your current feelings about your involvement (if any) in a religious organization and how—if at all—you'd like that to change.**

*My most positive experience with a religious organization was:*

*My most negative experience with a religious organization was:*

*About my current involvement, I feel:*

# Time at Home

**Young person is out with friends "with nothing special to do" two or fewer nights per week.**

**50% of youth surveyed have this asset in their lives.**

## Pros and Cons

<u>Focus:</u> **Youth debate the pros and cons of spending their evenings at home.**

**#73**

*You will need:*
• **writing paper or note cards**
• **pens or pencils**

Form two teams. Explain that the two teams will debate the asset of spending time at home. One team will advocate the importance of spending most evenings during a week at home with the family. The other team will advocate going out with nothing special to do as often as possible.

Have each team choose four debaters and one timekeeper. The rest of the team should help the debaters prepare. Let youth take notes as they get ready.

Flip a coin to see which team will go first. The first team then chooses a debater to present their position in two minutes. The timekeeper for that team signals when two minutes have passed.

Then the opposing team chooses one debater to present their position in two minutes. After each team has presented their position, the team that went first has their second debater present a one-minute rebuttal. Continue until all four debaters on each team have had an opportunity either to present or rebut.

As a group discuss the debate. Ask:

• **What were the strongest arguments in favor of each position?**

• **What are the benefits of spending most evenings at home? What are the drawbacks?**

• **Did this debate make you rethink how much time you spend at home? Why?**

• **What advice would you give parents or teens to make evenings at home more appealing?**

## Balancing Act

<u>Focus:</u> **Youth balance balloons to symbolize how much time they spend at and away from home.**

**#74**

*You will need:*
• **seven long, skinny balloons for each pair of young people**

Have each youth find a partner. Give each pair seven long, skinny balloons to inflate. Have partners decide who will do this activity first. Explain that the other partner is to hand the balloons, one at a time, to the person going first. Each balloon represents one night of the week. The person going first must hold the balloon in her or his left hand if the balloon represents a night of unstructured recreation (like going to a movie or playing pickup basketball with friends at a gym) or in the right hand if the balloon represents time spent at home or in a structured activity (such as music lessons or religious activities).

Have youth start with Sunday. If the first youth stayed home last Sunday evening, he or she holds the balloon in the right hand. If the youth had play practice on Monday night, he or she must hold the second balloon in the right hand without dropping the first. Go through the seven days of the week and see how well the youth holds the balloons. (If the youth has a balanced life in terms of structure and recreation, he or she should be able to hold all the balloons.) Repeat the activity for the other partner.

Take a quick poll of whether people had to hold most of their balloons in the left or right hand, or if most people had the balloons balanced. Then ask:

• **How would you rate the balance of your life in the past week? Was it a normal week? Explain.**

• **Is it easier for you to err in being too busy or not having enough to do? Why?**

• **Would you like for your life to be more balanced? Why or why not?**

• **What can you do to get your life more balanced?**

## Time Spent

How much time do you spend at home? Designate one weekday and one weekend day for each set of clocks. Then shade in the hours you typically spend at home for that day. Think about what you're doing during that home time. Are you sleeping? Eating? Hanging out? How much of that time is spent alone? With family?

# Weekday:_____

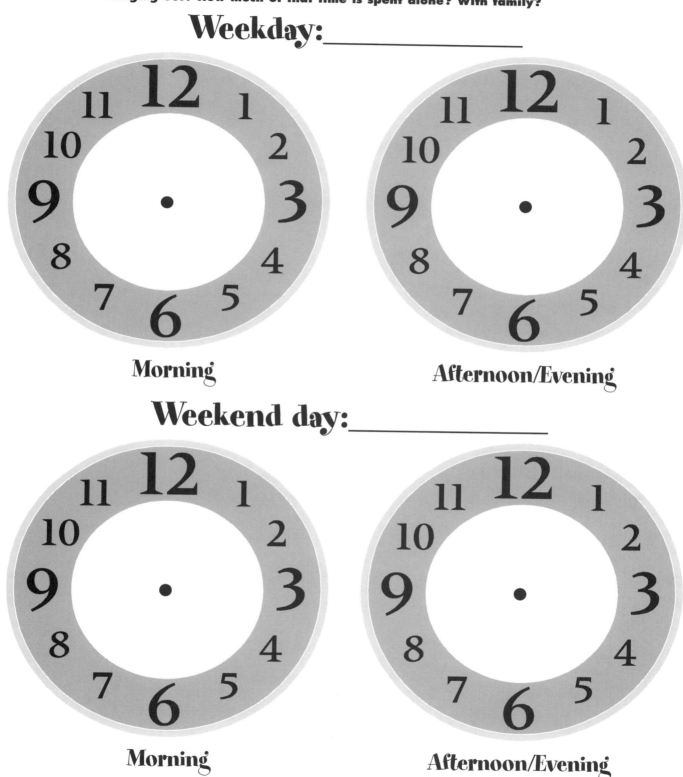

Morning          Afternoon/Evening

# Weekend day:_____

Morning          Afternoon/Evening

# PART 3

# Internal Assets

# Chapter 7

# Commitment to Learning

A commitment to learning, both now and in the future, is an important asset for youth. Search Institute identifies five "commitment to learning" assets. The activities in this chapter encourage youth to think about the importance of learning and of setting long- and short-term goals for themselves.

# Achievement Motivation

**Young person is motivated to do well in school.**
**21% of youth surveyed have this asset in their lives.**

## Motivating Walk

**Focus:** Youth experience and discuss the difference between encouragement and discouragement.

**#76**

**You will need:**
- some type of blindfold for each pair of youth
- newsprint and a marker or
- chalkboard and chalk

Ask each youth to find a partner. Give each pair a piece of cloth or a handkerchief to use as a blindfold. Have one person blindfold the other. On newsprint or a chalkboard, write: "Keep telling your partner that he or she can't do it as you lead her or him around the room. Don't give any encouragement."

Aloud, say something like: "We're now going to have the seeing partners lead the blindfolded partners from one end of the room to the other. Begin now."

Observe what happens. After everyone has moved the length of the room, stop the activity. On the chalkboard or newsprint, write: "This time, give your partner lots of support and encouragement."

Aloud, say something like: "Okay, let's do this activity again. Begin."

After everyone has moved to the other part of the room, stop the activity and have youth remove their blindfolds. Gather the group together and ask questions such as these:

- **What were you thinking as you were being led around the room?**
- **Which time was easier for the blindfolded youth? Why?**
- **How did it feel to get only negative feedback? Only positive?**
- **How did it feel to give only negative feedback? Only positive?**
- **Which is more motivating: negative or positive feedback? Why?**
- **What type of feedback do most youth get about school? What impact does it have?**
- **What are some things that are most motivating to you in school and learning?**

## Thinking About Teachers

**Focus:** Youth talk about ways teachers motivate and discourage them.

**#77**

Have youth form teams of three according to the first letter of their first name (for example, Anita, Arthur, and Andrea). Have the teams talk about the teachers they've had who have motivated them the most and what those teachers did to make them feel motivated.

After everyone has had the chance to talk, ask each team to report on ways teachers have motivated them. Then have youth form new teams of three according to the first letter of their last name (for example, Anderson, Aimes, and Appleby). Have the teams talk about teachers who discouraged them (without naming the teachers' names) and what those teachers did—or didn't do—that was so not motivating. Ask teams to report on ways teachers discouraged them.

Finally, after everyone has contributed to the discussion, have youth form new teams of three according to the last letter of their last name (or example, Jackson, Talen, and Lincoln). Have youth talk about how they motivate themselves to do well in school and additional techniques they could use to keep motivated. Share some of those ideas in the large group.

**Bumper Sticker Messages**

Create two bumper stickers with messages about doing well in school. See the examples for some ideas.

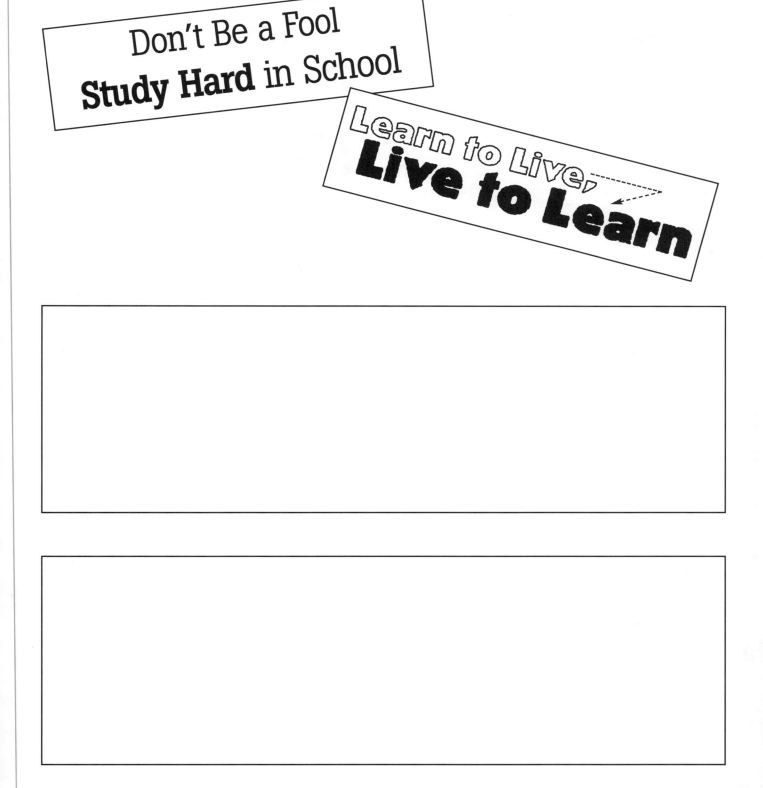

Don't Be a Fool
**Study Hard** in School

Learn to Live,
**Live to Learn**

# School Engagement

**Young person is actively engaged in learning.**
**64% of youth surveyed have this asset in their lives.**

## What's Great?

**Focus:** Youth tell what engages them about different aspects of their school.

**#79**

**You will need:**
- one matchbook for each group of youth

Have youth form groups of three or four. Give each group a book of matches. Say: "I'm going to name something specific about school. After I name the specific thing, the person holding the book of matches should take out one match, close the match cover, light the match and name aloud as many positive or engaging things about that aspect of school he or she can think of before the match burns out or needs to be blown out. While this is happening, the person to the right of the person with the lit match will count the items named. For example, I might say 'English,' and a person might say reading, learning more about authors, talking to the teacher, writing a short story, and so on. When you finish, give the matchbook to the person on your right and wait for me to name another specific aspect of school."

Name specifics such as these: after-school activities, lunch, science, study hall, and all-school assemblies.

Afterward, discuss questions such as:

- **How did you feel as you were doing this activity? Why? At what other times do you feel like this at school?**
- **How difficult was it to name a lot of different positive or engaging specifics? Why?**
- **Were you surprised by any of the responses you heard from other people?**
- **How did you feel holding the match, knowing that someone was counting your responses?**
- **What would make your school more engaging? Why?**

## The Best of the Best

**Focus:** Youth reveal their favorite classes and teachers.

**#80**

Have youth all crouch on the floor. Explain that they're going to be like a kernel of popcorn. When you ask a question, they should pop up (when they feel ready to do so) and shout out their answer before crouching down again.

Begin by asking each youth to name their favorite school subject. After youth take turns shouting out their answers ask them to name their favorite teachers. (If you are a teacher, suggest that youth should not name you, even if you are one of their favorites.) After that, ask youth to name the best class they have ever taken.

Then bring the group together and discuss questions such as these:

- **What makes a teacher a good one?**
- **How does a good teacher make learning exciting and fun?**
- **What is/was so great about your favorite class?**
- **What about learning is most exciting to you?**
- **How can you get excited about learning when the subject or teaching method seems boring?**

## Learning Acrostic

Create an acrostic for the word "learning" that reflects the importance of being engaged in learning. For example, if you did an acrostic for the word "school," you might write something like:

**S**tudy regularly
**C**all for help when you need it
**H**ighlight main points
**O**ffer suggestions
**O**bserve deadlines
**L**earn as much as you can

**L**
**E**
**A**
**R**
**N**
**I**
**N**
**G**

# Homework

**Young person reports doing at least one hour of homework every school day. 45% of youth surveyed have this asset in their lives.**

## Homework Centers

<u>Focus:</u> **Youth imagine and design an ideal study hall.**

**You will need:**
- **a large sheet of newsprint or other paper— one for each group of three youth**
- **markers**

Ask youth to form teams of three according to their favorite meal of the day (e.g., form a team with one person who enjoys each meal). Give each threesome a piece of paper and some markers. Have each team draw what an ideal study hall would look like. Encourage youth to be creative and include such details as types of furniture and illustrations of how people are behaving.

After teams finish, have them hang their pictures on the wall and explain why they included the items that they did. Then ask:

- **What are things you identified that make homework productive? What interferes?**
- **Is it important to have time each day to focus on doing homework? Why or why not?**
- **How many of these things are available to you right now?**
- **What could you do to make your homework time more productive?**

## Brainstorm Clouds

<u>Focus:</u> **Youth brainstorm ways to encourage themselves to do homework.**

**You will need:**
- **chalkboard and chalk or**
- **newsprint and a marker**

Draw a huge cloud on a chalkboard or newsprint. Ask youth to brainstorm as many ideas as they can that would encourage them to do homework or would help make it easier for them to do homework. (Remind youth that the purpose is to give as many ideas as possible and that there are no bad ideas.)

After you finish, ask:

- **Which of the ideas do you like the most? The least? Why?**
- **If a friend asked you for help in figuring out how to do homework better, what advice would you give?**
- **How do you feel about the time you spend doing homework? Is it too much? Not enough? How's your concentration?**
- **What keeps you from doing homework?**
- **What motivates you to do homework?**

## Homework Pie

**#84**

**Think about the time you spend on homework each week. Is it at least one hour or more per school day? (Or about five or more hours each week?) Why or why not? Of the time you do spend on homework, divide the pie below to show about how much of your homework time you spend on each subject.**

**After you finish, ask yourself:**

• **On which subject do I spend the most time doing homework? Why?**

• **For which subjects do I not do any homework? Why?**

• **Is the balance of how I spend my homework time good? How could it be better?**

• **Should I be doing more homework? Less? Is the time I spend about right? Why?**

• **How do I feel about my homework habits right now?**

• **How can I improve my homework habits?**

**Number of hours spent doing homework each week: _____**

# Bonding to School

**Young person cares about her or his school.**
**51% of youth surveyed have this asset in their lives.**

## The Benefits of Caring

**Focus:** **Youth demonstrate how caring and uncaring behavior affects their attitudes about school.**

**#85**

Form two groups of youth and separate the groups from each other. Quietly talk with one group so that youth from the other group can't hear. Say that you want each person to choose an affirming comment to make, such as "You're great" or "I like your smile." Encourage them to make it personal, such as using "I" and "you" words, and suggest that each person choose a different comment.

Then quietly talk with the other group so that youth from the first group can't hear. Say that you want each one to think of a discouraging comment to make, choosing one of the following: "Stop that," "Is that the best you can do?" "I don't like that." (If you add other comments, make sure they aren't hurtful in personal ways.)

Then explain to both groups that you want the two groups to break up and mingle around the room. When you say, "Stop," each person should pair up with someone nearby and say their discouraging comment to the other person. Each time you say "stop," youth should find new partners and repeat the same messages they chose originally.

Do the activity four or five times. Then bring everyone together and ask questions such as these:

- **Which people did you enjoy talking with? Why?**
- **Which people did you not enjoy exchanging comments with? Why?**
- **How does the way people at your school interact with each other affect your feelings about your school?**
- **Overall, do you care about your school? Why or why not?**
- **Why are students more apt to care about their schools when they're in positive, encouraging environments?**

## School Ratings

**Focus:** **Students evaluate how they feel about their school.**

**#86**

**You will need:**
- **five sheets of newsprint**
- **a marker**
- **masking tape**

Write each of these sentences on a separate sheet of newsprint:
"I am really proud to go to my school."
"I care about my school and I try to make it the best place to be."
　"All schools are the same."
　"If I had a choice, I would still go to my school."
　"Most students overrate my school."

Hang these sheets around the room. Form five teams of about equal size. Give each team a marker and station them each at a different piece of newsprint.

Have teams discuss their opinions of the sentence on their sheet to see if they can come to a consensus of whether they agree or disagree with it and why. Then have them write "True," "False," or "Controversial" if they can't agree as a group. Have them write their answers on the newsprint along with a one-sentence explanation before moving to the next newsprint to the left. When all the teams have responded to all the statements, identify statements about which there was wide agreement or disagreement. Ask:

- **Why do people have different feelings about their schools?**
- **What makes a school a place for students to care about?**
- **What ideas do you have to make your school a better place to be?**
- **Is it important for students to feel good about their school? Why or why not?**
- **If you could create the ideal school, what would it be like? Why?**

## Your School

What do you enjoy most about your school? What makes you care about your school? On each pencil below, write one thing that you like about your school.

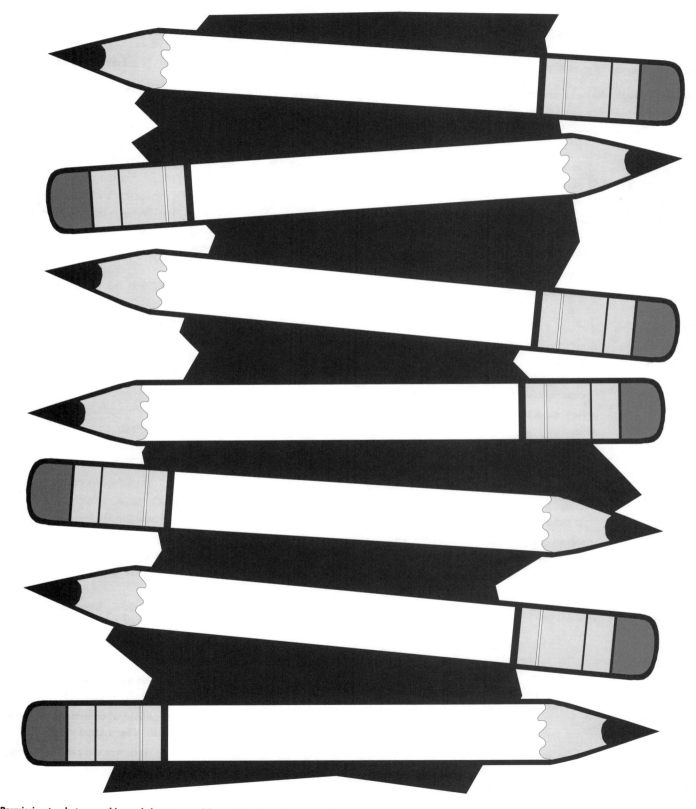

# Reading for Pleasure

**Young person reads for pleasure three or more hours per week.**
**24% of youth surveyed have this asset in their lives.**

## Oodles of Reading

**Focus:** Youth discuss what they usually read for pleasure.

**#88**

**You will need:**
- news-papers
- magazines
- books
- comic books

**H**ave four reading stations set up around the room. Have one station contain only newspapers. Have another have only magazines while another has books and the last area has comic books.

Have youth go to the station of the type of reading they do most. Give them a few minutes to browse through what's there. Then have youth rotate so that they spend a few minutes in each area. Then have the whole group discuss questions such as these:

- **Which type of material do you most enjoy reading? Are there other types of reading materials that interest you? What are they?**
- **How much time each week do you spend reading for pleasure?**
- **Overall, how do you feel about reading? Why?**
- **Who reads a lot in your household?**
- **Do you spend more time each week reading things that someone else chooses or that you get to choose? Why?**
- **Do you wish you could spend more time reading things you enjoy? Why or why not?**
- **Why do you think reading for pleasure is an asset?**

## Different Books for Different Folks

**Focus:** Youth think about exploring different types reading.

**#89**

**H**ave youth take off their shoes and place them in a pile in the center of the room. Have youth form a circle around the shoes. When you tell them to start, have youth keep trying on different shoes until they find a pair that fits—and isn't the pair that they came in with.

After youth finish, ask questions such as these:
- **How did it feel to try on other people's shoes?**
- **What surprised you about trying on different shoes?**
- **What did you think of the shoes that fit you?**

Then say something like: "Sometimes we have a set idea of what we most like. But sometimes we need to try something new to see what might fit that we didn't expect. The same is true for reading. Sometimes we think we enjoy reading only comic books or comic strips. Or we may think we enjoy only novels but not poetry."

Have youth brainstorm various kinds of reading that may be worth considering. Then ask:
- **What kinds of reading seem most interesting or appealing?**
- **What kinds of reading are you sure you're not interested in?**
- **What criteria do you use when deciding types of reading material to choose?**
- **How do you know when a reading choice really fits you—like a good shoe?**
- **What are some different types of reading you'd like to try?**

## #90 Your Favorite Books

Think about the best books you've ever read in your life (even include those you read when you were much younger). Write the names of those books on the top four books below. On the books on the bottom of this page, write the names of three books you would like to read in the future.

# Chapter 8

# Positive Values

Holding strong, positive values is an important foundation upon which healthy choices are made. Empathy, personal convictions, and commitments to the welfare of others shape the kinds of people we become. Search Institute identifies six positive values that serve as assets. The activities in this chapter are designed to help build these values.

**Asset #26**

# Caring

**Young person places high value on helping other people.**
**43% of youth surveyed have this asset in their lives.**

## Helping Hands

**Focus:** Youth recall ways they have helped others and have been helped by others.

**You will need:**
- three or four pieces of colored construction paper for each youth
- markers or pens

Give each youth three or four pieces of colored construction paper. Have them trace their hands on the paper and cut as many hands as they can out of the pieces. On some hands, have youth write about recent incidents where they helped someone else. On the other hands have youth write about incidents when they appreciated help from someone else.

After youth finish, have them describe some of what they wrote, then hang their hands on a wall so they form a collage. Ask:

- **What are some of the most positive experiences you've had helping or caring for someone? What did you learn from those experiences?**
- **What feelings do you get when someone helps and cares for you?**
- **What are some positive experiences you've had being helped by others?**
- **Sometimes we get so preoccupied that we don't think about helping others. What can we do to remember the value of helping and caring for others?**

## Caring for Others

**Focus:** Youth identify and prepare to do a caring project.

**You will need:**
- one sheet of paper for each group of four youth

Before doing this activity, figure out how many youth are in your group. Divide that number by four and get that many sheets of paper. On each sheet of paper, write one group or issue that would benefit from having youth help, such as: the environment, elderly people, animals, children, families, or singles.

Have youth form teams of four. Give each foursome a sheet of paper with a category on it. Ask each team to identify three caring projects they could do that would help this group of people or cause. For example, youth could pick up trash in a community park one weekend day. They could take a group of younger children swinging and sliding for an hour. Youth who can drive could run some errands for an elderly person.

Once youth finish selecting projects, have the teams report back to the group. Have the group discuss whether they want to do one project or form smaller teams to do a number of projects. Set goals for doing these projects. During your discussion, ask questions such as:

- **What are some reasons you selected the project or projects that you did?**
- **What are the most important things to consider when planning a helping project?**
- **In addition to the service you will provide, what else might you expect to learn or gain from doing this project?**

**INTERNAL ASSETS: POSITIVE VALUES**

**#93**

## Helping Coupons

Think of three people you would like to help, and write one name on each of the coupons below. Then write one way you could help on each of the coupons.

For example, you might write: Dad—Help wash the dishes; or: Susan—Tutor her in math one hour this week. Be creative, and add your own designs to the coupons. After you write them, give them to the appropriate people and let them know you will be available to help them when they need it.

### COUPON

For:_____

I can help by:_____

### COUPON

For:_____

I can help by:_____

### COUPON

For:_____

I can help by:_____

# Asset #27 Equality and Social Justice

**Young person places high value on promoting equality and reducing hunger and poverty.**

**45% of youth surveyed have this asset in their lives.**

## Pictures of Injustice

<u>Focus:</u> **Youth respond to pictures that represent injustice**

**#94**

**You will need:**

- **five magazine or newspaper photos that depict injustice**
- **five Post-it Notes® for each youth**

Find five magazine or newspaper photographs that illustrate injustice (both domestic and international) and hang them around the room. For example, find pictures that show poverty, acts of violence, acts of discrimination, and so on.

Give each youth five removable adhesive notes (such as Post-it Notes®). Ask youth to look at each picture, then write a one-sentence response to the picture on the note, then post their sentence near the photograph. Encourage youth to remain silent while they do this activity.

Give youth time to go back and read what others wrote. Then ask:

- **How did you feel looking at these photographs? Why?**
- **Which photograph had the most impact on you? Why?**
- **What did you think about what other people wrote? Why?**
- **Did you want to do something about what you saw? What could you do? Why?**
- **How do you feel about injustice? Why?**

## Pizza Party

<u>Focus:</u> **Youth simulate the inequitable distribution of food in the world.**

**#95**

**You will need:**

- **four cups of cooked rice**
- **at least two slices of pizza for each youth**
- **colored paper**
- **scissors**
- **money for pizza**

Before doing this activity, count the number of youth in your group, and divide that number by six. Cut strips of one color paper equal to that number. Then cut strips of a different colored paper so that you have enough strips for each youth to get one piece of paper. For example, if you have 24 youth, 4 of them will get strips of yellow and the other 20 will get strips of green.

Have youth each chip in two or three dollars for a pizza party. Order so that each youth could have at least two pieces. Be sure to give each youth a strip before the pizza is ordered. (Before the pizzas are to arrive, have ready four cups of cooked rice.)

Have everyone sit together according to the color of their strips of paper. Once the pizzas arrive, give all of the pizzas to the smaller group. Give the larger group only rice. Then tell everyone to enjoy their food.

Watch what happens for about five minutes (make sure the group that has the pizza doesn't actually eat more than two pieces each). Then stop the activity. Let everyone eat pizza while you discuss questions such as these:

- **What was your reaction when you saw how the pizza was being distributed?**
- **How did you feel paying the same amount for a little rice as other people did for a lot of pizza?**
- **How did you feel having lots of pizza when you knew most people had only a little bit of rice?**
- **Analysts have found that one-sixth of the world's population eats most of the world's food while the rest of the world practically starves. What do you think about that?**
- **What can we do to help end hunger? What should we urge business, government, and other institutions to do?**

## #96  That's Not Fair!

**When it comes to social injustice, the United States has made a lot of progress in some areas and little in others. Check your opinions about each of the issues below. Feel free to check as many different answers as you feel apply to each situation.**

| Issues | I am really concerned about this | We've made a lot of progress | We still have a lot to do | This injustice is overblown |
|---|---|---|---|---|
| 1. Racial discrimination | ____ | ____ | ____ | ____ |
| 2. Gender discrimination | ____ | ____ | ____ | ____ |
| 3. Poverty | ____ | ____ | ____ | ____ |
| 4. Sexual orientation discrimination | ____ | ____ | ____ | ____ |
| 5. Hunger | ____ | ____ | ____ | ____ |
| 6. Ethnic/cultural discrimination | ____ | ____ | ____ | ____ |
| 7. Religious discrimination | ____ | ____ | ____ | ____ |
| 8. Age discrimination | ____ | ____ | ____ | ____ |
| 9. Disability discrimination | ____ | ____ | ____ | ____ |
| 10. Class discrimination | ____ | ____ | ____ | ____ |

# Integrity

**Young person acts on convictions and stands up for her or his beliefs.**

**63% of youth surveyed have this asset in their lives.**

## Opinions Count

**Focus:** Youth assert their beliefs by writing a letter to an editor or other media person.

**#97**

**You will need:**
• writing paper
• pens

Explain that one way to stand up for what you believe is to speak out. Encourage youth to choose a movie, TV show, magazine article, newspaper article, or some other media or story about which they have a strong opinion. They can either agree or disagree with the story or its presentation.

Help them find out to whom to address the letter. Then work with youth in crafting a non-attacking, provocative letter about their opinion. Encourage youth to use "I" statements and to be specific about their concerns.

Ask for volunteers to read what they wrote to the group before mailing their letters. Then ask:
• **What are things about which you are most likely to take a stand? Why?**
• **What is the hardest part of being assertive about your beliefs?**
• **What are some things you do that help you be assertive?**

Youth can choose to send their letters to the local newspaper (or school paper) as a letter to the editor, especially if the story they're writing about just happened, or they can send their letter to the actual author, editor, or producer of the story. If some of the letters are published, display them prominently in your classroom or meeting area.

## Classroom Continuum

**Focus:** Youth stand on a continuum based on their own experience being assertive.

**#98**

**You will need:**
• masking tape
• two sheets of paper
• a marker

Put a piece of masking tape on the floor of your classroom or meeting room from one end to the other. At one end, hang a sign that says "Agree." On the opposite end, hang a sign that says "Disagree."

Tell youth that you're going to read a series of statements. Youth are then to stand on a place along the continuum that best reflects their true experiences. Encourage youth to be honest and say what really happens, not what they wish would happen.

Read statements such as these (or others that fit):
• **When someone says something I disagree with, I tell that person how I feel.**
• **I talk through issues with somebody before making a decision.**
• **When someone hurts me, I tell the person.**
• **When a clerk gives me too much change, I tell the clerk.**
• **It's easier for me to state my opinion around strangers than around friends or family.**
• **I feel my family accepts me when I have a differing opinion.**
• **I often compare viewpoints on subjects with my friends.**
• **I find it easy to stand up for what I believe.**

When you finish, come together and ask:
• **Did you find yourself more often agreeing or disagreeing with the statements I read? Or were you in the middle a lot?**
• **When are times that it's most important to be assertive? When is it less important?**
• **If a friend is having a hard time asserting her or his beliefs or choices, how can you help her or him be more assertive?**

**#99**

## A Model of Integrity

It's easier to act on your convictions and stand up for your beliefs when you have role models who do the same. Think about an adult in your life whom you admire for her or his integrity. In the space below, write a letter to that person, expressing what you admire about that person and why. Then thank the person for being a good example. After you finish, consider sending it to the person.

*Dear* _____,

# Honesty

**Young person "tells the truth even when it is not easy."**
**63% of youth surveyed have this asset in their lives.**

## 20 Questions

**Focus:** Youth simulate honesty and lying.

### #100

Have youth form groups of three. Have one person from each group leave the area so you can talk to them privately. Explain that these people will have the role in the group of "liar." Each group is going to play 20 questions where one of the members will ask a series of questions about a word, trying to figure out what it is. The word the person will be trying to figure out is "penguin." Explain that their role as liars is to sometimes lie, giving the person incorrect answers at times and correct answers at other times. Have those youth rejoin the group.

Then ask for a different person from each of the threesomes to join you away from the area so that others can't hear you. Explain that they will have the role of being totally honest. Explain how to play the game and that the answer is "penguin." Tell them that they must always give the correct answer. Have those youth rejoin the group.

Explain that all the groups will be playing 20 questions. In this activity, the third person in each group (the one who has not been assigned a role) will ask a yes or no question of the two others in the group. After getting their answers, the person then asks another question, up to 20. The goal is to try to figure out the answer before all 20 questions are used up.

Let the groups begin. After they finish, have everyone come back together. Ask questions such as:

- How did it feel to ask questions and get answers that weren't always consistent? What did you think was going on?
- How did it feel to be the person always telling the truth? Why?
- How did it feel to be the person who sometimes lied? Why?
- Is it important to be honest? Why?

## Fudging the Truth

**Focus:** Youth discuss small lies.

### #101

**You will need:**
- a chalkboard and chalk or
- newsprint and a marker

Have youth get into groups of three or four. Say: "Telling the truth gets trickier when we know we can hurt someone's feelings by telling the truth. Oftentimes, it's easy to tell small lies that we may tell to be polite."

Explain that youth are to discuss within their groups what they would do in each of the situations you list on the chalkboard or on newsprint. List situations such as these:

- A friend who has been gaining weight and is upset about it asks you if you think he or she's getting fat.
- A classmate has been making a pottery bowl and has redone it 10 times. It still looks crooked to you, and he or she wants to know if you think it's now straight.
- A friend bought a new jacket that he or she just loves. You think it looks awful. Your friend wants to know what you think.
- A relative you like gives you a sweater for a gift. It fits, but you really don't like the style.

Then bring youth together and discuss questions such as these:

- How difficult is it to tell the truth in these situations? Why?
- Do you always tell the truth? Why or why not?
- Is it easier for you to be honest with some people than others? Why?
- If you value honesty does it mean you should never lie? Why or why not?
- What if you lie and feel guilty about it? What should you do?
- What does it mean to value honesty?

**#102**

## Your Honesty Policy

Companies and organizations create policies that document what people should do in certain situations. Think about how much you value honesty and why. In the space below, write an honesty policy that describes what you would do if you were asked to be dishonest, what you would do if you found it hard to tell the truth, and what you would do if you told a lie.

HONESTY POLICY

# Responsibility

**Young person accepts and takes personal responsibility.**
**60% of youth surveyed have this asset in their lives.**

## Taking Charge

**Focus: Youth role-play responsibility.**

**You will need:**
• several sections of newspaper

Ask for four volunteers to participate in a role play. Talk with these four youth away from the rest of the youth so others don't hear. Ask one youth to refuse to accept and take responsibility. Ask another youth to refuse to accept responsibility but then take responsibility after the fact. Ask a third youth to accept responsibility but then not act on it. And have the last youth accept and also act on being responsible. Explain that you want the four volunteers to take some newspapers, walk in front of the rest of the group, and begin wadding up the papers and throwing them all around the room. Then when you ask them questions, you want each one to give an answer that fits with their role. Explain that you also want the two who are to take responsibility to clean up the mess after you leave.

Give them time to make a mess. After they've done this a while, say: "What a mess! Who is going to accept responsibility and clean this up?" Allow each youth to answer. Say: "Well, I want you all to clean this up." Then walk away while two of the youth clean it up.

Then bring everyone together to discuss the following:

• Who took the most responsibility? How?
• Who took the least responsibility?
• What are important aspects of personal responsibility? Why?
• What gets in the way of your accepting and taking responsibility?
• In which areas of your life would you like to accept and take more responsibility? Why?
• Which person did you have the most respect for in this situation? The least amount of respect? Why?

## Character Comparison

**Focus: Youth compare a responsible person with an irresponsible person.**

**You will need:**
• newspapers, newsmagazines, and magazines such as *People*— one of each for each group of youth

Have youth form groups of five or six. Give each group a newspaper, a newsmagazine, and a magazine like *People*. Have groups each find one story about a person who took responsibility and another story about a person who didn't take responsibility.

Have groups each identify similarities and differences between the two people, including their attitudes, actions, and personality traits. (If the stories don't give that much information about the individuals, allow groups to take some creative license into what they think these people are really like based on the stories.)

Then have groups report on their people to the full group. Ask questions such as these:

• **Is it easier to find news stories about responsible people or irresponsible people? Why?**
• **What did you admire most about the responsible person you studied? Why?**
• **Do you think it would be easy or hard for you to act on that trait that you most admired? Why?**
• **Who are some other responsible people you admire? What about them do you admire?**

**#105**

## Places of Responsibility

You can accept and take responsibility in all areas of your life. Complete each of the statements below, naming at least one way you can take responsibility in each area.

I can take more responsibility
at home by: _____
_____

I can take more responsibility
at school by:_____
_____

I can take more responsibility
in my community by:_____
_____

I can take more responsibility with my friends by:
_____
_____

I can take more responsibility with my personal
goals by: _____
_____

**Asset #31** # Restraint

**Young person believes it is important not to be sexually active or to use alcohol or other drugs.**

**42% of youth surveyed have this asset in their lives.**

## Listening to the Lyrics

**Focus:** Youth analyze the messages about sex, alcohol and other drugs in music lyrics.

*You will need:*

- **tapes or compact discs of music popular with young people**
- **a stereo on which to play them**

Choose songs on tapes or compact discs that have lyrics that pertain to sex, alcohol, or other drugs. (To be sure the songs are appropriate for your youth, preview them in advance. Also try to find songs that address all three areas of sex, alcohol, and other drugs.) Play a song for the class. Ask youth to listen closely to the words. After it is finished, ask questions such as these:

- **What does this song say about sex, and/or alcohol, and other drugs?**
- **How typical is this message compared to other music you hear?**
- **How much do you think your friends agree with this message? Why?**
- **How much do music lyrics influence your values about sex, alcohol, and/or other drugs?**
- **Do females and males get different messages about sex, alcohol, and other drugs? Why do you think this is the case?**

Play another song and repeat the activity and questions. Do this for a number of songs, then ask these summary questions:

- **Many people believe it is important for teenagers to abstain from sex, alcohol, and other drugs. What are reasons for this perspective?**
- **Why do many teenagers choose to abstain from sex, alcohol, and other drugs? Why do others choose to get involved with sex, alcohol, and/or other drugs?**
- **Do you think it's important for teenagers to value abstaining from sex, alcohol, and other drugs? Why?**
- **How can youth support each other in choosing to abstain?**

## Well, I'd Never!

**Focus:** Youth talk about their values and reasons why they would never do certain things.

Have youth get into pairs. Say: "We're going to have a contest to see who can name the most things they would never do. The rules are that the things have to be possible, you can't repeat what your partner has already said, and you have to alternate between serious and silly topics."

Then have the pairs begin. When all the pairs are finished, ask:

- **What are some of the silly things people said they wouldn't do?**
- **What are some of the serious things? (If no one mentions sexual activity or alcohol or other drug use, ask if anyone mentioned these things in their discussions.)**
- **What are some reasons behind your deciding not to do some of the serious things? (If youth need prompting, mention safety, parents' wishes, personal values, laws, religious beliefs.)**
- **What are ways youth support or pressure each other in these areas?**
- **What are some ways to respond to negative pressures?**

INTERNAL ASSETS: **POSITIVE VALUES**

**#108**

The asset of restraint says it's better for teenagers to wait until they're adults to have sexual intercourse, to use alcohol responsibly at the legal age, and never to use other drugs. Under each category, list three reasons why you think it's important for teenagers to have restraint in these areas.

## Three reasons to abstain from sexual activity as a teenager

**1**

**2**

**3**

## Three reasons to not drink alcohol as a teenager

**1**

**2**

**3**

## Three reasons not to use drugs

**1**

**2**

**3**

# Chapter 9

# Social Competencies

Social competencies are some of the important personal strengths and skills young people need to negotiate the maze of choices and options they face. These assets lay a foundation for independence and competence as youth become adults. This chapter offers ideas for building five social competency assets identified by Search Institute.

# Asset #32 Planning and Decision Making

**Young person knows how to plan ahead and make choices.**

**29% of youth surveyed have this asset in their lives.**

## Decision Road Map

**Focus:** Youth experience the advantages and drawbacks of getting help from others in making decisions.

### #109

**You will need:**

- three road maps
- pens or pencils

Place three road maps in different parts of the room. Form three teams and have each team choose a home base point on the map and a destination.

Encourage teams to find as many different routes as possible to get from their home base to their destination. Keep track of how many they come up with. Ask youth to discuss why they like or dislike each route. Finally, have them settle on one route.

When teams finish, ask:

- **What were things that happened on your team that helped you find lots of routes?**
- **Was it harder or easier to pick a route as a team than it would be to do it by yourself? Is the route you picked better because more people were involved?**
- **When you have to make decisions in your life, in what ways can it help to have input from others?**
- **In addition to getting feedback from others, what are things you do that help you make decisions?**

## Toothpick Challenge

**Focus:** Teams of youth search for a marked toothpick to illustrate the value of planning.

### #110

**You will need:**

- two boxes of toothpicks
- two tables

Before doing this activity, buy two boxes of toothpicks. In each box, make a tiny mark on one toothpick. Put the marked toothpicks back into the boxes.

Form two teams. Have one team come with you away from the group. Show that team one box of toothpicks and explain that there is one toothpick inside that has a mark on it. Explain that the two teams will have a race to find the marked toothpick. Encourage this team to find the toothpick now and plan a strategy for how to find it before the other team during the race.

After the team finishes planning its strategy, have them put the toothpicks back into the box and give the box to you.

Return to the rest of the group. Explain to both teams that you have two boxes of toothpicks. Say that the first team to find the toothpick that looks different wins. When you say "Search!" simultaneously dump the two boxes, one on a table to your left and one on a table to your right. When both teams have found the marked toothpick, ask questions such as these:

- **One team planned ahead of time. How much did that planning help?**
- **What were some strategies the two teams used? How did they work?**
- **Do you usually have more success when you plan ahead or when you "wing it"? Why?**
- **Can planning ever be negative? If so, how?**
- **What kinds of planning skills would you like to develop? How might you get started?**

**INTERNAL ASSETS: SOCIAL COMPETENCIES**

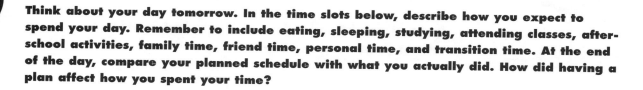

## Daily Planner

**#111**

Think about your day tomorrow. In the time slots below, describe how you expect to spend your day. Remember to include eating, sleeping, studying, attending classes, after-school activities, family time, friend time, personal time, and transition time. At the end of the day, compare your planned schedule with what you actually did. How did having a plan affect how you spent your time?

## Day of the Week _____

|  | Plan | What I Actually Did |
|---|---|---|
| **Midnight** |  |  |
| **1 a.m.** |  |  |
| **2 a.m.** |  |  |
| **3 a.m.** |  |  |
| **4 a.m.** |  |  |
| **5 a.m.** |  |  |
| **6 a.m.** |  |  |
| **7 a.m.** |  |  |
| **8 a.m.** |  |  |
| **9 a.m.** |  |  |
| **10 a.m.** |  |  |
| **11 a.m.** |  |  |
| **Noon** |  |  |
| **1 p.m.** |  |  |
| **2 p.m.** |  |  |
| **3 p.m.** |  |  |
| **4 p.m.** |  |  |
| **5 p.m.** |  |  |
| **6 p.m.** |  |  |
| **7 p.m.** |  |  |
| **8 p.m.** |  |  |
| **9 p.m.** |  |  |
| **10 p.m.** |  |  |
| **11 p.m.** |  |  |

Asset#33

# Interpersonal Competence

**Young person has empathy, sensitivity, and friendship skills.**
**43% of youth surveyed have this asset in their lives.**

## Paper Bag Skits

<u>Focus:</u> **Youth perform and talk about skits on relationships.**

**#112**

*You will need:*
* **paper bags filled with an assortment of items— one bag for each group of youth**

Have youth form teams of five. Give each team a paper bag filled with unrelated items such as: keys, an onion, a postage stamp, a handkerchief, a bar of soap, a spoon, a spool of thread, a facial tissue, a marker, a rubber band, a sticker, a coupon, a penny, and others. Make the contents of each bag unique.

Explain that each team is to develop a skit to perform in front of the entire group using all the items from their bag. The skit must emphasize what's important in forming a relationship with someone.

Give youth time to work on their skits and present them to the group. Then ask:

* **What were some of the key messages about forming relationships in the skits?**
* **What did you learn about building relationships through the process of developing your skit?**
* **Is building relationships easy or difficult? Why?**
* **If you were doing these skits to show other youth tips for developing relationships, what key points would you make?**

## Active Listening

<u>Focus:</u> **Youth practice active listening skills with each other.**

**#113**

*You will need:*
* **chalkboard and chalk or**
* **newsprint and markers (optional)**

Explain that people are more willing to form relationships when they feel that they're not being judged and that someone really cares about them. Dr. Thomas Gordon, the author of *P.E.T.: Parent Effectiveness Training* (Penguin Books, 1970), gives a number of relationship-building tips based on what he calls "active listening." You may want to write these on a chalkboard or newsprint:

* Use "I" messages instead of "you" messages (e.g., "I feel sad," "I like your approach," "I hear you saying you're angry").
* Encourage the person to speak by responding with "Tell me more," or, "How did you feel when that happened?"
* Name feelings that the person is trying to express. "That made you angry," or, "You're sad that he broke up with you."
* Listen with empathy.

Ask youth to form teams of three. Ask each team to think of a topic about which they have strong feelings. Have two people in each team practice active listening skills. Ask them to discuss the topics they chose while the third observes and responds at the end by saying what they did well and where they could improve. Repeat the activity two more times so youth each have a turn being the observer. Afterward, ask:

* **What are some things that happened when you tried active listening?**
* **How did it feel to try these techniques? What was awkward? Helpful?**
* **If these techniques became natural to you, what benefits would you see in using them with other people?**
* **In addition to active listening, what are other ways you can build relationships with people?**

INTERNAL ASSETS: SOCIAL COMPETENCIES

## Your Relationship Skills

People tend to be good at some relationship skills and not as good at others. Rate yourself on a scale from one to five on several aspects that are important in developing a relationship. (Be honest!) Five is for skills you feel you have developed very well, and one is for skills you think you need a lot of work on. At the end of the list, add some other relationship skills that you think are important.

   After you finish, circle one of the skills that you gave a low rating and that you would like to work on. After a week, check your progress.

## Skills

## Rating

| | Needs work | | | | Well developed |
|---|---|---|---|---|---|
| Initiating conversations with someone you don't know very well. | 1 | 2 | 3 | 4 | 5 |
| Calling someone on a regular basis. | 1 | 2 | 3 | 4 | 5 |
| Asking someone her or his opinion on an issue. | 1 | 2 | 3 | 4 | 5 |
| Telling someone when he or she hurts your feelings. | 1 | 2 | 3 | 4 | 5 |
| Doing something you have in common with someone. | 1 | 2 | 3 | 4 | 5 |
| Listening to a person when he or she needs to talk. | 1 | 2 | 3 | 4 | 5 |
| Telling someone how you really feel about her or him. | 1 | 2 | 3 | 4 | 5 |
| Complimenting someone for something he or she did that you liked. | 1 | 2 | 3 | 4 | 5 |
| Doing something nice for someone because you feel like it. | 1 | 2 | 3 | 4 | 5 |
| Hanging out with someone because you like the person. | 1 | 2 | 3 | 4 | 5 |
| _____ | 1 | 2 | 3 | 4 | 5 |
| _____ | 1 | 2 | 3 | 4 | 5 |
| _____ | 1 | 2 | 3 | 4 | 5 |
| _____ | 1 | 2 | 3 | 4 | 5 |

# Cultural Competence

**Asset #34**

Young person has knowledge of and comfort with people of different cultural/racial/ethnic backgrounds.

34% of youth surveyed have this asset in their lives.

INTERNAL ASSETS: SOCIAL COMPETENCIES

## A New Taste

**Focus: Youth share examples of their cultural heritage.**

Ask youth to bring in some food, a piece of clothing, a game, a knickknack, information about a ritual, or something else that represents their cultural heritage. Have youth take turns sharing what they brought in and explaining (or demonstrating) its cultural significance. For example, a youth with Swedish heritage may bring in an almond and talk about the tradition of hiding the almond in rice pudding (a dessert) before it is served. The person who gets the nut is supposedly the next person to marry. Oftentimes, the person who gets the nut also receives a small gift. (If you have a large group, you may want to form smaller groups for sharing.)

Afterward, ask questions such as these:

- **How do you feel about your cultural heritage? Why?**
- **How important is your cultural heritage to you? Why?**
- **How does your family acknowledge your cultural heritage?**
- **Why do you think cultural competence is an asset?**
- **Are there some cultural things we have in common in the United States? What are some examples?**
- **Which cultures or representations of cultures were particularly interesting to you?**

**Variation**

Invite someone to your group who can offer a specific cultural experience. Some examples include inviting someone to bring snacks from a particular culture or asking a religious leader to bring samples of what people eat during certain holidays; asking someone to teach a folk dance; or inviting your music teacher to lead your class in a song in a different language. Ideally, the heritage of the person coming to class should include the culture he or she is representing.

## Out vs. In

**Focus: Youth play a game that illustrates exclusivity and inclusiveness.**

Have youth form a circle. Ask youth who are right-handed to stay in the circle and for all the left-handed youth to leave the circle. Have the right-handed circle members lock arms tightly. Explain that the object of this activity is for the outsiders to try to break into the circle. If someone succeeds, he or she joins the group and then chooses someone within the circle to leave.

Do the activity for a while. Afterward, ask:

- **How did it feel to be part of the circle and try hard not to let others in? Why?**
- **How did it feel to be an outsider? Why?**
- **How did it feel to be part of the circle and then asked to leave without any apparent reason? Why?**

Repeat the activity. This time have all the brown-eyed youth form a circle and hold hands. Have all the other youth stand outside the circle. Explain that when someone from the outside wants to join the circle, he or she should gently tap the shoulder of someone in the circle and ask to join in. Whenever those in the circle are asked, they are to open up their arms and let the people in.

Do the activity, then ask:

- **How did you feel about this activity compared to the first? Why?**
- **Why is it good to get to know people who are different from us?**
- **What one thing can you do to expand the circle of people you know and with whom you feel comfortable?**

**#117**

## Contact with Other Cultures

How much contact do you have with people of other races, ethnic backgrounds, and cultures? In the inventory below, check the amount of contact you have had with people of other cultures.

| Type of contact | Weekly | Monthly | Annually | Once in a while | Never |
| --- | --- | --- | --- | --- | --- |
| See people with different cultural backgrounds in my community | ❑ | ❑ | ❑ | ❑ | ❑ |
| Talk to people with cultural backgrounds that are different from mine | ❑ | ❑ | ❑ | ❑ | ❑ |
| See television shows that positively portray people with different cultural backgrounds | ❑ | ❑ | ❑ | ❑ | ❑ |
| Listen to music from other cultures | ❑ | ❑ | ❑ | ❑ | ❑ |
| Hear others talk positively about people from different cultures | ❑ | ❑ | ❑ | ❑ | ❑ |
| Eat foods from other cultures | ❑ | ❑ | ❑ | ❑ | ❑ |
| Study in school about people with a variety of cultural backgrounds | ❑ | ❑ | ❑ | ❑ | ❑ |
| Read positive stories about people from many different cultures | ❑ | ❑ | ❑ | ❑ | ❑ |
| Attend cross-cultural events | ❑ | ❑ | ❑ | ❑ | ❑ |

# Resistance Skills

**Young person can resist negative peer pressure and dangerous situations.**
**37% of youth surveyed have this asset in their lives.**

## Resisting Danger

**Focus:** Youth observe positive and negative peer pressure.

**#118**

**You will need:**
- one blind-fold

Ask for one volunteer who is willing to be blindfolded to leave the room. With the rest of the group, set up a maze of obstacles with chairs, desks, and other objects in the room. Make sure the maze has a fairly wide walkway. Explain that when you come back with the volunteer, that person will be blindfolded and youth are to yell out advice that will get the volunteer to bump into objects.

Leave the room. Tell the volunteer that you're going to blindfold her or him. Explain that he or she will be going through an obstacle course blindfolded and that he or she needs to listen to you as you whisper advice on which way to go.

Return to the room. Start the activity. Stay close to the volunteer and constantly whisper good advice.

Afterward, take the blindfold off the volunteer and bring the group together to discuss:

- As the volunteer, who did you trust at first? Why? Who did you learn to trust? Why?
- Why did you eventually resist doing what the masses were saying?
- How hard was it to listen to me once you figured out that most people were pressuring you to make wrong turns?
- How was this activity similar to what it's like to try to resist peer pressure and dangerous situations? Why?
- How can having strong resistance skills be helpful to you?

## The Power of Resistance

**Focus:** Youth identify various ways to resist peer pressure and dangerous situations.

**#119**

**You will need:**
- pieces of candy

Ask for two volunteers. Have one volunteer be the "pressurer" and the other person be the one who gets pressured. Give the pressurer some candy. Tell the volunteer who is to be pressured to do everything in her or his power to resist taking or eating any of the candy. Have the rest of your group observe what happens.

Start the activity. Tell the pressurer to use any kind of verbal tactic to get the person to take or eat some of the candy. Watch what happens. Then tell the pressurer to use physical force without hurting the person.

After a brief while, stop the activity. Then ask for another volunteer. Have that volunteer help the person physically being pressured to resist that pressure. Start the activity again with the pressurer trying verbal and physical tactics to get the person to eat the candy.

After you finish, ask questions such as these:

- What did the person do to resist taking and eating the candy?
- What was most effective? Least effective? Why?
- What happened when the pressurer starting using physical force?
- Why is it important to ask for support when you feel you can't resist pressure by yourself?
- What types of pressure do you face as teenagers? Who pressures you?
- What do you do to resist these pressures?

**#120**

## Say Yes to Saying No

Sometimes it's easy to get caught up in the moment. You intend not to do something and then you feel pressured to do it. To keep that from happening, write 10 creative ways to say no. If you wish, share your ideas with friends.

1 _____

2 _____

3 _____

4 _____

5 _____

6 _____

7 _____

8 _____

9 _____

10 _____

# Peaceful Conflict Resolution

**Young person seeks to resolve conflict nonviolently.**
**44% of youth surveyed have this asset in their lives.**

## Peacemakers Around Us

**Focus:** Youth create a mural of peacemakers and research qualities of these peacemakers.

On a large piece of paper, have youth draw pictures, hang up photocopies of peacemakers pictured in books, or write the names of peacemakers they know in their communities, their countries, and the world—both living and dead. (Examples of peacemakers include Martin Luther King Jr., Mother Teresa, Nelson Mandela, Elie Wiesel, Mikhail Gorbachev, the Dalai Lama, Bishop Desmond Tutu, and Albert Schweitzer. Consult the latest edition of *The World Almanac* for a list of Nobel Peace Prize winners if you would like to find more or study people youth may not know much about.)

Form groups of three or four. Have each group choose one peacemaker to research. (If the peacemaker is a local person, have the group visit and interview that person.) Once groups finish their research, have them report their findings to the group.

Then discuss questions such as these:

* **Why are peacemakers important to our community and to the world?**
* **How do people in conflict with peacemakers tend to respond to peacemakers? How do peacemakers usually respond to that? Can you think of specific examples?**
* **What's difficult about being a peacemaker? Why?**
* **What can we do to support peacemakers?**
* **How can you be more of a peacemaker?**

**You will need:**
* **a large piece of newsprint or other paper**
* **markers or crayons**
* **access to a photocopy machine**

## Dealing with World Conflict

**Focus:** Youth study countries in conflict and suggest peaceful resolutions.

Take out a world map. Have youth identify places in the world that are at war with each other or are in the midst of civil wars. (If youth have trouble identifying places, bring copies of the international section of a newspaper or newsmagazine for them to look through.) Assign each war or conflict to a group of youth and explain that they are mediators. Each group should form two teams, one representing each side of the conflict.

Have youth find out more about the conflict through newspapers, magazines, and other sources of information. Youth should research how long the conflict has been going on and why it originally started. Have each side within each group state the problem as they see it. Then have both sides make a list of two or three solutions that would satisfy them. Then have the sides work together until they can decide on a solution that is mutually satisfying.

Once groups agree to a solution, ask:

* **How difficult was it to state the problem from your perspective? Why?**
* **How difficult was it to think of two or three solutions to suggest? Why?**
* **How difficult was it to find one solution that was mutually satisfying?**
* **Why do you think wars can drag on so long without a peaceful resolution?**
* **Is it ever difficult for you to resolve conflicts in your own life? Why?**
* **Think about someone with whom you have had a conflict. What's one thing you can do to try to peacefully resolve that conflict?**

**You will need:**
* **a current world map**
* **newspapers, magazines, and other sources of information about current events**

**#123**

## Rewriting Your History

Think about a time in your past when you found yourself involved in a major conflict. Write about that situation, answering the questions below.

1. What was the conflict about?

2. What was my view of the situation?

3. What was _____'s view of the situation?

4. Did we resolve the conflict? Why or why not?

5. If I had this conflict now, what would I do differently? Why?

6. Which of the following peaceful conflict resolution skills would I like to strengthen? (Check all that apply and star the one to work on first.)

❑ Listen to the other person more and understand that person's position.

❑ Take time to deal with my emotions rather than taking them out on the other person.

❑ Be clear about my needs and opinions by using "I" messages.

❑ Brainstorm lots of ideas to resolve the conflict.

❑ Improve my problem-solving skills.

❑ Expect gradual improvements with some setbacks, not miraculous, sudden improvements.

❑ Be sincere.

❑ Care for the person even though we're in conflict.

# Chapter 10

# Positive Identity

Growing up includes developing a set of personal attitudes that help you function as an independent, competent person. These attitudes shape the way you look at yourself, the world, and the future, and help you succeed in the challenges you face. Search Institute has identified four positive identity assets that focus on young people's view of themselves—their own sense of power, purpose, worth, and promise. Activities for building these assets appear in this chapter.

# Personal Power

**Young person feels he or she has control over "things that happen to me."**
**45% of youth surveyed have this asset in their lives.**

## Disaster Control

<u>Focus:</u> **Youth decide how best to cope with a difficult situation.**

Have youth form groups of three or four. Explain that each group lives near a river and heavy rains have suddenly come, flooding the area. Working together as a group, each group must choose only three items that they think would best help them cope in the situation. They can choose any three items they would like.

Give groups time to work. Then have groups report their three items. Discuss the following questions:

- **How did having the opportunity to choose any three items help you in this difficult situation? Why?**
- **How would you have felt if I told you that you could do nothing and just needed to let the flood damage your homes and community?**
- **When bad things happen, do you usually feel you have some choice and power to deal with the situation? Why or why not?**
- **Is it important to have personal power? Why or why not?**

## Pointing Fingers

<u>Focus:</u> **Youth name sources of good events and bad events.**

**You will need:**
- **three sheets of newsprint**
- **a marker**

Hang newsprint on different sides of the room. Label one, "My responsibility; my fault"; another, "Someone else's responsibility; someone else's fault"; and the third, "Pure luck; pure chance." Clear the area between the sheets so that youth can freely move among them.

Explain that you will name situations and that youth are to run to the newsprint that best describes the probable cause of the event. Name both positive and negative situations, giving youth time to move around.

Sample situations: You get an A in history. You don't get invited to a party. You run for student council and don't win. You get the lead in the school play. You study hard and still fail a test. Someone steals your bike. You earn a scholarship.

Gather youth together. Say: "Martin Seligman has done research on personal power and says it's important to take responsibility and correct our behavior when things go wrong because of our choices, and also see that bad things can happen to us that are not our fault. When we fail, we need to realize that we all make mistakes and we're all learning. When bad things happen that are beyond our control, we need to recognize that we're in a difficult situation but that we are not 'at fault.' Seligman also says that when good things happen to us, it's good to interpret those events globally. For example, if you get an A in math, it's better to think that you're smart overall rather than just smart in math or that you got lucky. When bad things happen, Seligman says it's better for our identity to be specific about our interpretation. For example, if someone you're dating breaks up with you, it's better to believe that that person doesn't want to date you, rather than that nobody likes you."

Then ask:
- **When is it easier to feel you have control in life: when bad things happen or good things? Why?**
- **How does society teach us to interpret positive events? negative events?**
- **Do you think some people have more personal power than others? Why?**
- **In what ways can you have more personal power?**

# #126  A Powerful Memo

In business, people write memos all the time to send important messages. In the space below, write a memo to yourself about your personal power. In the first paragraph of the message, critique your current attitude about your personal power. In the second paragraph, name two specific things you can do to have more personal power.

**Date:** _____

**To:** _____

**From:** _____

**Subject:** *Your personal power* _____

**Message:**
_____
_____
_____
_____
_____
_____
_____
_____
_____
_____
_____
_____
_____
_____
_____
_____
_____
_____
_____
_____
_____

**Date:** _____

**To:** _____

**From:** _____

**Subject** _____

**Messa** _____

# Self-Esteem

**Young person reports having high self-esteem.**

**47% of youth surveyed have this asset in their lives.**

## Messages

**Focus: Youth analyze messages about self-esteem found in magazine advertisements.**

**You will need:**

- an assortment of magazines aimed at teenagers

**B**ring in magazines that appeal to teenagers. Make sure you have some that generally are targeted to males as well as some that generally are targeted to females. Have youth form teams of three and discuss what the magazine ads say about self-esteem. Have teams discuss questions such as these:

- **Overall, do the ads in these magazines imply that most young people have high or low self-esteem? Why do you think that is?**
- **What are the messages about self-esteem for males? Females? Is there a difference? Why do you think that is?**
- **Why does advertising work?**
- **Is it easy or hard to believe an ad? Why?**
- **Do you feel better or worse about yourself now that you've looked at the ads? Why?**
- **What can you do to develop or nurture a strong sense of self-esteem for yourself and your friends?**

## Self-Esteem Notes

**Focus: Youth affirm each other by writing positive messages.**

**You will need:**

- scissors
- one sheet of red construction paper for each youth
- safety or straight pins—one for each youth
- a pen or pencil for each youth

**H**ave each youth cut a large heart out of the construction paper. Ask youth to help each other pin their hearts to their backs.

Ask youth to walk around the room and write something positive on each person's heart. For example, youth might write: "I like your smile," or "You're a great listener," or "I admire your ability to do well in math."

After youth finish writing, have them help each other take off their hearts. Give youth time to read their messages. Ask:

- **What are some of the messages you got today that really give you a boost?**
- **How did it feel to take time to affirm other people?**
- **What was it like writing positive messages to others, knowing that people were writing positive messages on your heart?**
- **How important is it to affirm other people?**
- **What are ways youth can enhance their own self-esteem and the self-esteem of their friends?**

**#129**

## What's Great About Me

Think about what you like about yourself. Then read the words below. Circle the ones that describe you. (Don't be shy! Circle as many words as you want.) Add your own words if there are some you feel are missing.

Healthy   Decisive   Frank
Musical   Carefree   Patient
Responsive   Direct
Active   Dependable   Loving
Creative   Thoughtful   Independent
Quiet   friendly   Quick
Determined   Responsible   Open-minded
Sensitive   Intelligent   Patient
Jovial   Enterprising   Leader
Sympathetic   Resourceful
Proud   Helpful
flexible   Social   Patriotic   Relaxed
Understanding   Investigative   Predictable
Practical   laid-back   Driven
Inquisitive   Hard-working   Ethical
Talkative   Moral   Imaginative
Honest   Kind   Stimulating

# Sense of Purpose

**Young person reports that "my life has a purpose."**
**55% of youth surveyed have this asset in their lives.**

## Passionate People

**Focus:** Youth interview people who find meaning through their interests and passions.

Have each youth identify an adult in his or her extended family, neighborhood, school, or other organization to interview. Explain that the purpose of the interview is to find out what gives the person meaning in life.

Before youth do the interviews, brainstorm a list of four or five questions that will help youth find out what makes the person really tick. Some sample questions might include: What do you really enjoy doing? What activities get you really excited? If you could choose one thing to do with your time, and not need to worry about money or other responsibilities, what would you do? What gives you meaning in life? Why?

Have youth conduct their interviews and then share what they found out with the rest of the group. Then ask:

- **Was it easy for this person to articulate how he or she finds meaning in life? Why or why not?**
- **Do you think most people know what gives them purpose? Why or why not?**
- **What gives you purpose?**
- **If you're not sure what gives you purpose, how can you find out?**
- **Do you think it's important for people to have a sense of purpose? Why or why not?**

## Redefining Success

**Focus:** Youth identify ways people search for success and meaning.

**You will need:**
- **chalkboard and chalk or**
- **newsprint and a marker**

As a group, brainstorm a list of ways people search for success and meaning. Examples might include money, fame, a loving family, achievement, and awards. After you finish, ask:

- **Are these things bad? Why or why not?**
- **Which do you think is better: a person who wants to make lots of money and chooses a lifestyle that makes a lot of money or a person who chooses what he or she wants to do and then—just by doing what he or she does really well—makes a lot of money? Why? What about people who do what they want and never make much money at all?**
- **What's difficult about finding meaning in life?**

Then read this quote by author Joseph Campbell to the group. "You have a success in life, but then just think of it—what kind of life was it? What good was it that you've never done the thing you wanted to do in all your life? I always tell my students, go where your body and soul want to go. . . . Follow your bliss and don't be afraid, and doors will open where you didn't know they were going to be."

Ask:
- **How hard is it to find "bliss" or "purpose" in life? Why?**
- **What keeps people from finding "bliss" or "purpose"?**
- **If I asked you if you knew what your purpose was in life, could you tell me? Why or why not?**
- **What would you need to do to find out (if you don't know) or take the next step toward achieving it (if you do know)?**

## A Meaningful Gift

The things we enjoy doing and the things we have talent for are what give us meaning in life. And what gives us a personal sense of purpose is also our gift to others and our society. In other words, you are a personal gift to the world. On the gift tag below, write as many things you can think of that give you meaning in life, that you have a talent for, and that you have to give others.

# Positive View of Personal Future

**Young person is optimistic about her or his personal future.**
**70% of youth surveyed have this asset in their lives.**

## A Look to the Future

**Focus:** Youth create collages representing their futures.

On a large sheet of paper, have youth create a group collage of what they think the future will look like. Encourage them to cut out pictures and words from magazines, catalogs, and newspapers to glue onto the paper.

After youth finish, have them explain their work. Then ask questions such as:

**You will need:**
- **a large sheet of paper**
- **magazines, catalogs, and newspapers**
- **glue**
- **scissors**

- **How different do you think your life in the future will be from what it is like now? Why?**
- **What kinds of things do you worry about in the future? What are some things that really give you hope?**
- **How can you prepare for the future so that it will be exciting and positive?**

## Nudge Your Neighbor

**Focus:** Youth answer questions about the kind of future they hope for.

Have youth form teams of four and sit in a tight circle (their knees should be touching as they sit with their legs crossed). Have teams answer the questions below (write them on the chalkboard or newsprint). Have one person designated to start answering each question. That person must speak and then elbow the person on her or his right to signal that it's that person's turn. Continue until everyone has answered the question. Then the team should address the next question.

**You will need:**
- **chalkboard and chalk or**
- **newsprint and a marker**

Use questions such as these:

- **What will your financial situation be like in the future?**
- **What will your family be like in the future?**
- **What kind of career, if any, do you think you'll pursue in the future? Why?**
- **What kind of education do you need so that you can pursue the career you want?**
- **Where do you think you'll live in the future?**
- **Which issues will you be most concerned about in the future?**
- **What will be your biggest challenges in the future? Why?**
- **How do you expect to deal with what the future presents to you?**

**#135**

## Your Dream of Your World

On August 28, 1963, Martin Luther King Jr. gave his famous "I Have a Dream" speech in Washington, D.C. The message was clear: King had a positive view of his future, and he was optimistic.

In the space below, write a short message of your dream for the future. Do like Dr. King. Don't get caught up in disturbing events that may surround you.

# Dream big. Dream positively. Dream with optimism.

# Additional Asset-Promoting Resources from Search Institute

## Resources for Understanding Assets

### All Kids Are Our Kids: What Communities Must Do to Raise Caring and Responsible Children and Adolescents

*by Dr. Peter L. Benson*

In his new book, Dr. Benson presents a comprehensive vision of what children and adolescents need to grow up healthy and what everyone in a community must do to rebuild this foundation for healthy development. This book offers an in-depth exploration of "developmental assets" that all kids need and outlines a vision for creating healthy communities for children and adolescents. Published by Jossey Bass.

#300                              $24.95 plus shipping

### Starting Out Right: Developmental Assets for Children

*by Dr. Nancy Leffert, Dr. Peter L. Benson, and Jolene L. Roehlkepartain*

With this report, Search Institute offers new frameworks for understanding and building the foundation that children from birth through age 11 need to begin a healthy life. It offers valuable new insights and includes useful charts and detailed descriptions.

#364                              $14.95 plus shipping

### Profiles of Student Life: Attitudes and Behaviors

Hundreds of schools and dozens of community-wide initiatives across the United States use data from this survey to develop asset-building strategies and to create new visions for their youth. This survey focuses on grades 6 through 12 and looks at the assets young people need to grow up healthy. Cost depends on number of students surveyed.

## Ideas for Building Assets

### 150 Ways to Show Kids You Care

This unique handout inspires and motivates adults with practical ideas for showing kids they care.

#355                       $9.95 packet of 20 plus shipping

### Creating Intergenerational Community: 75 Ideas for Building Relationships Between Youth and Adults

*by Jolene L. Roehlkepartain*

This booklet offers 75 easy ideas that are perfect for anyone or any group wishing to build relationships between youth and adults.

#670                              $4.95 plus shipping

### 101 Asset-Building Actions

Full-color poster

A 22" x 30" full-color, glossy poster, *101 Asset-Building Actions* is an ideal way to display and reinforce the asset message. Perfect for any office, classroom, meeting room, or as a gift for others who care for or about kids.

#340                              $8.95 plus shipping

### Assets: The Magazine of Ideas for Healthy Communities and Healthy Youth

This full-color newsmagazine offers information and strategies for promoting positive youth development and building developmental assets in kids. Published quarterly, *Assets* explores new areas in youth development research and shows how you can use this research in your work or life. Includes a *Clip and Use* page, *Ideas That Work*, and much more. $14.50 for four issues. To subscribe, call 1-800-869-6882.

## Free Information

### Source Newsletter

This free, eight-page newsletter highlights the latest Search Institute research on children and youth. Each issue explores a different theme, presenting scientific data in nontechnical language and suggesting implications for people who work with children and youth.

### Resource Catalog

This free catalog shows the latest Search Institute resources available. You'll find materials on assets, parent education, healthy communities, youth development, service learning, youth programs, sexuality education, middle school improvement, prevention, religious youth work, training opportunities, presentation offerings, and surveys.

## About the Author

Jolene L. Roehlkepartain is a writer and editor who specializes in parenting and education issues. She is the author or coauthor of a dozen books and curricula for educators, parents, youth, and youth workers, including *Starting Out Right: Developmental Assets for Children* (Search Institute, 1997), *Fidget Busters* (Group Publishing, 1992), and *Surviving School Stress* (Teenage Books, 1990). She has worked with children and youth for 17 years and lives in Minneapolis, Minnesota.

## About Search Institute

Search Institute's mission is to advance the well-being of adolescents and children by generating knowledge and promoting its application through research and evaluation, publications and practical tools, and training and technical assistance. The institute collaborates with others to promote long-term organizational and cultural change that supports the healthy development of all children and adolescents.

# 40 Developmental Assets

**Search Institute has identified the following building blocks of healthy development that help young people grow up healthy, caring, and responsible.**

## Type

## Asset Name and Definition

**External**

### Support
1. **Family support**—Family life provides high levels of love and support.
2. **Positive family communication**—Young person and her or his parent(s) communicate positively, and young person is willing to seek parent(s') advice and counsel.
3. **Other adult relationships**—Young person receives support from three or more nonparent adults.
4. **Caring neighborhood**—Young person experiences caring neighbors.
5. **Caring school climate**—School provides a caring, encouraging environment.
6. **Parent involvement in schooling**—Parent(s) are actively involved in helping young person succeed in school.

### Empowerment
7. **Community values youth**—Young person perceives that adults in the community value youth.
8. **Youth as resources**—Young people are given useful roles in the community.
9. **Service to others**—Young person serves in the community one hour or more per week.
10. **Safety**—Young person feels safe at home, at school, and in the neighborhood.

### Boundaries & Expectations
11. **Family boundaries**—Family has clear rules and consequences, and monitors the young person's whereabouts.
12. **School boundaries**—School provides clear rules and consequences.
13. **Neighborhood boundaries**—Neighbors take responsibility for monitoring young people's behavior.
14. **Adult role models**—Parent(s) and other adults model positive, responsible behavior.
15. **Positive peer influence**—Young person's best friends model responsible behavior.
16. **High expectations**—Both parent(s) and teachers encourage the young person to do well.

### Constructive Use of Time
17. **Creative activities**—Young person spends three or more hours per week in lessons or practice in music, theater, or other arts.
18. **Youth programs**—Young person spends three or more hours per week in sports, clubs, or organizations at school and/or in community organizations.
19. **Religious community**—Young person spends one or more hours per week in activities in a religious institution.
20. **Time at home**—Young person is out with friends "with nothing special to do" two or fewer nights per week.

**Internal**

### Commitment to Learning
21. **Achievement motivation**—Young person is motivated to do well in school.
22. **School engagement**—Young person is actively engaged in learning.
23. **Homework**—Young person reports doing at least one hour of homework every school day.
24. **Bonding to school**—Young person cares about her or his school.
25. **Reading for pleasure**—Young person reads for pleasure three or more hours per week.

### Positive Values
26. **Caring**—Young person places high value on helping other people.
27. **Equality and social justice**—Young person places high value on promoting equality and reducing hunger and poverty.
28. **Integrity**—Young person acts on convictions and stands up for her or his beliefs.
29. **Honesty**—Young person "tells the truth even when it is not easy."
30. **Responsibility**—Young person accepts and takes personal responsibility.
31. **Restraint**—Young person believes it is important not to be sexually active or to use alcohol or other drugs.

### Social Competencies
32. **Planning and decision making**—Young person knows how to plan ahead and make choices.
33. **Interpersonal competence**—Young person has empathy, sensitivity, and friendship skills.
34. **Cultural competence**—Young person has knowledge of and comfort with people of different cultural/racial/ethnic backgrounds.
35. **Resistance skills**—Young person can resist negative peer pressure and dangerous situations.
36. **Peaceful conflict resolution**—Young person seeks to resolve conflict nonviolently.

### Positive Identity
37. **Personal power**—Young person feels he or she has control over "things that happen to me."
38. **Self-esteem**—Young person reports having high self-esteem.
39. **Sense of purpose**—Young person reports that "my life has a purpose."
40. **Positive view of personal future**—Young person is optimistic about her or his personal future.